Steve Caplin

Adobe

3D Photoshop®
imagine · model · create

Steve Caplin

This Adobe Press book is published by Peachpit, a division of Pearson Education.

For the latest on Adobe Press books, go to www.adobepress.com.

To report errors, please send a note to errata@peachpit.com.

Copyright © 2014 by Steve Caplin

Acquisitions and Project Editor: Rebecca Gulick
Production Coordinator: Maureen Forys, Happenstance Type-O-Rama
Copyeditor: Liz Welch
Designer, Compositor, and Indexer: Steve Caplin
Proofreader: Patricia Pane

ISBN-13: 978-0-321-95655-2
ISBN-10: 0-321-95655-9

9 8 7 6 5 4 3 2 1

Printed and bound in the United States of America

Foreword

PHOTOSHOP IS THE ULTIMATE PLAYGROUND for creative people to share their artistic vision, develop their style, or learn new tools that enhance their creative expressions.

Almost all digital artworks have some element of depth and dimension. Whether you choose to show this depth using real 3D models or 2D images with an added perception of depth (faux 3D), the end result adds realism and completes the message you, the designer, are trying to convey.

The concepts laid out in this book provide an understanding of what can be accomplished using 3D tools in Photoshop. Working with real 3D objects allows you to easily change your mind about position, lighting, perspective, or even the actual shape of the object. Further, you can easily change how something looks by manipulating the materials of a 3D model and have it respond accurately and realistically to the light. This is very much like working in a real photography studio, where the subject can be repositioned, the lighting can be changed, and the camera angles can be manipulated to help communicate the final look. The advantage is that all of this can be done post-processing and you have the flexibility to change your mind at any point.

Steve Caplin's approach in this comprehensive book on all things 3D in Photoshop allows you to get started right away with the creation of 3D models. As you work through each of the chapters, you begin to build your knowledge of important 3D concepts and learn what is possible utilizing the tools. The book is filled with rich imagery and many simple tutorials along the way that are fun to explore and easy to get through.

It's rare that I come across a true Photoshop expert – Steve Caplin has an incredible depth of knowledge with all of Photoshop. He has been working with the 3D tools from the start and is one of the few experts who understands how to leverage the 3D capabilities in order to push his creative ambitions forward and create stunning and eye-catching artwork. This book will give you a firm understanding of 3D in Photoshop by giving you a thorough look at what's possible.

Zorana Gee
Adobe Photoshop Senior Product Manager

Contents

Acknowledgments

I'm immensely grateful to the following:

Digimation, Inc (www.digimation.com), for allowing me to use their outstanding 3D models

Keith Martin, for helping me to develop the keyboard shortcuts font

Calvin Holmes, for asking me about animation during a lecture

David Asch, for help and support

My wife, Carol, for her encouragement and tolerance

…and of course Adobe Systems, Inc, for making the best software on the planet.

About this book

THIS BOOK WON'T TEACH YOU how to use Photoshop. It's too big a subject, and it's beyond the scope of a book that's exclusively about 3D modeling. I've assumed that you already have a reasonable working knowledge of Photoshop, and that you're familiar with terms such as Layer Masks, Smart Objects and Layer Styles. If this isn't the case, then I'd like to direct you to one of my other books, *How to Cheat in Photoshop*, which should be enough to help you out of any difficulties you may encounter along the way.

This book was written with Photoshop CC in mind. Most of the techniques here will work equally well with Photoshop CS6, except for certain of the references to combining, separating and instancing 3D objects in Part Three. I've indicated on the relevant pages where techniques can only be used with Photoshop CC.

Most of the techniques can equally well be used by owners of Photoshop CS5 as well, although there were a number of significant interface changes between that version and CS6, which means that many of the dialogs will look very different. In particular, the controls for extruding, revolving and inflating 3D objects used a separate dialog called Repoussé in CS5, which was done away with entirely in CS6 and beyond.

Most of the 3D models used as examples in this book have been taken from websites on which they're freely available for download, and I've provided download links for all of them. Models I've made myself can also be downloaded, from the book's website at 3DPhotoshop.net.

3D modeling in Photoshop is a huge subject, and I haven't attempted an exhaustive examination of every tiny aspect of the system. There's just too much to go into, and most of it would bore all but diehard 3D modelers who need the ultimate in control over their scenes. Instead, you'll find everything you need to produce striking, vibrant models, and to combine them into spectacular scenes.

Introduction

SIX YEARS AGO I HATED 3D MODELING. All that business with NURBS and B-splines, with projections and lofting and sweeping, seemed far from the business of creating illustrations. 3D modeling, I was convinced, was the province of technicians and mechanics.

Then, in 2007, Photoshop CS3 appeared, and with it came the ability to import, move, light and render 3D objects. You couldn't create objects directly in the application, but you could import them from a variety of sources – including the free Google Sketchup. I played around with Sketchup for a while, using it to create items such as boxes and parallel shelf systems that would otherwise be tricky to draw directly in Photoshop, but I got no joy from it. Sketchup was then, and is today, a rather clumsy, fussy and occasionally downright pigheaded application that's really only good for creating architectural models for Google Earth (which is why Google bought it in the first place).

At the time, I was spending most of my working life producing photomontage illustrations for newspapers and magazines. When the *Sunday Telegraph* phoned up and said they wanted an illustration of a train jumping off the track, I was stumped. I had plenty of source images of trains – around 20 CDs full of the things, from my Corel photo library collection – but they were all of trains sitting neatly on their rails. To make the image work we'd have to be able to see the train from below, and that was impossible to photograph.

Then I remembered a book of 3D models published by Taschen, which I'd bought on a whim. It contained a couple of hundred high-quality rendered images of all kinds of everyday objects, with the bonus that all the objects were included on the accompanying DVD. So I dug it out, opened up a train model and placed it in Photoshop. And, of course, I was able to turn it around to view it from any angle I chose, adding carriages, low loaders and all the other elements I needed to complete the image – the added cars, politicians and business people who were the subject of the story. Suddenly, the whole point of including 3D models in Photoshop made sense to me.

As CS3 evolved into CS4, it brought with it the ability to wrap artwork around 3D primitives – and to generate not only 3D postcards, but real 3D objects from bump maps. It took a bit of getting used to: white is high, black is low, and the technique is very limited in what it's able to produce. But when I needed to build a compartmentalized museum case for a magazine illustration, it was clearly the easiest way to produce a perspective box.

Photoshop CS5 brought Repoussé, a 3D modeling environment whose name may have been short-lived (it didn't survive past CS5) but which enabled us to extrude, revolve and inflate 3D objects. The end results are much the same as we use today; the main difference with CS6 was that the process no longer took place within a separate modal dialog, and the head-up control system was now very much easier to use. Photoshop CC has brought a much better way of managing 3D layers, as well as much faster rendering and better previews of such components as lighting and shadows.

Because 3D modeling in Photoshop started in such a low-powered, rudimentary way, I've been able to stay on top of its development at each stage of the process. I'm no longer scared by 3D modeling, although the merest glance over the shoulder of someone using Cinema4D, Maya or 3ds Max is enough to send shivers down my spine. Being broken in gently is often the easiest way to keep up.

I recognize, though, that for anyone coming to 3D modeling in Photoshop from scratch, the whole process must seem like a minefield of unfamiliar terms. What's the difference between materials and texture? How do you work with normals and specularity? Why would you want to make a mesh from a depth map? There's a lot to figure out here.

The good news is that you don't need to study anything before you need it. Rather than bore you with a lot of science and theory, we're going to dive right in and start building 3D models on page one, chapter one. As each new technique is required we'll see how to make it work for us, and how to get the best out of it.

3D modeling in Photoshop used to be reserved for those users who had splashed out for the Extended (read: more expensive) version of Photoshop. Now, with Photoshop CC and the rest of the Creative Cloud, everyone gets access to all the 3D features. If you own a copy of Photoshop, then all these techniques are at your fingertips.

Although Photoshop offers a wide and powerful selection of 3D modeling tools, it's by no means comprehensive. If you want to model an airplane, or a car, or a faucet, or a tree, then you're better off learning one of the dedicated 3D programs I complained about at the beginning of this introduction: Photoshop simply can't compete on the same terms with these heavyweights. But if most of your work is in photomontage, and you need to introduce occasional 3D elements, then you may well find that Photoshop is all you need.

Steve Caplin
London, 2013

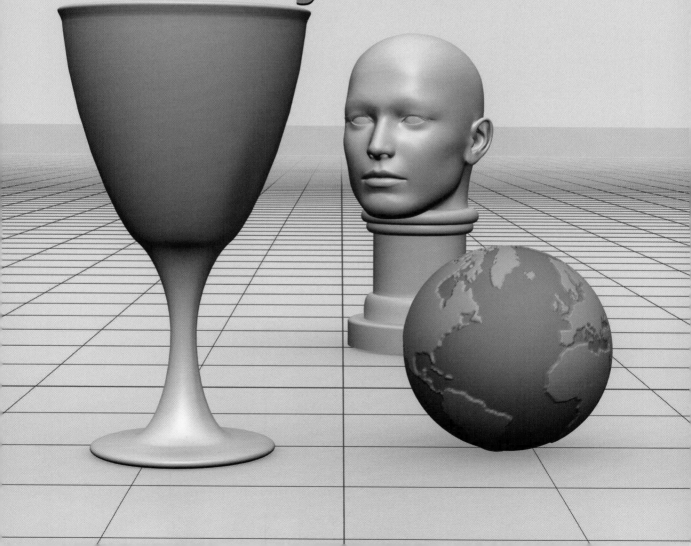

PART ONE
Making 3D objects

PART ONE
Making 3D objects

1 Making and moving a 3D object

THE BEST WAY TO LEARN about 3D modeling is to make your own 3D model. We'll start with a piece of simple text, and see how easy it is to extrude. This will turn it into a true 3D object that we can then spin around to view from any angle.

This chapter will look at the basics of handling, moving and rotating models, and working within the 3D environment. We'll also look at setting up the 3D workspace so that it's easier to view all the tools you need at a glance, without having to open and close separate panels.

First, though, let's begin by creating a new document and setting up a text object.

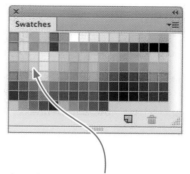

1 Start by making a new Photoshop document: about 1000 pixels square is a good size. You can work at any size you like, but at least 1000 pixels will allow you to make a 3D object you can see clearly and manipulate easily.

2 The default Photoshop colors are black and white, but you won't see your object very clearly if you make it black. In the **Swatches panel**, choose any color you like. I've picked this pale orange – you can see the shading better with lighter colors.

3 Next, use the **Type tool** to type some text – the word **3D** will do fine. Choose a sans-serif font, such as Myriad Bold (you can do this easily by typing the first couple of characters of the font's name in the Font field on the Options Bar). Press *Enter* to complete the text object.

Make the text good and big on your screen – use **Free Transform**, if you like, to enlarge the text layer, making sure you hold *Shift* as you drag a corner handle so you don't distort the letter forms.

Turning the text into 3D

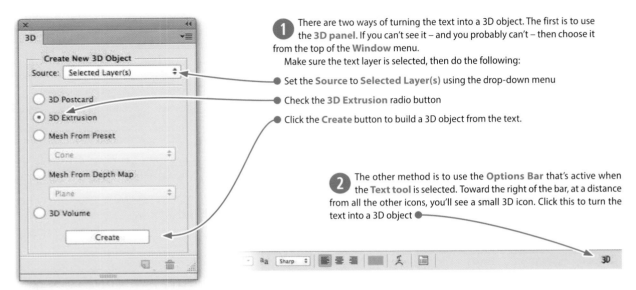

1 There are two ways of turning the text into a 3D object. The first is to use the **3D panel**. If you can't see it – and you probably can't – then choose it from the top of the **Window** menu.

Make sure the text layer is selected, then do the following:

- Set the **Source** to **Selected Layer(s)** using the drop-down menu
- Check the **3D Extrusion** radio button
- Click the **Create** button to build a 3D object from the text.

2 The other method is to use the **Options Bar** that's active when the **Text tool** is selected. Toward the right of the bar, at a distance from all the other icons, you'll see a small 3D icon. Click this to turn the text into a 3D object

3 In an instant, your text will be turned into a real 3D object. You'll notice the view change to show 3D-specific items: the **Ground Plane**, the base your object sits on, and the **Secondary View** in the top-left corner, which shows the same object from a different angle.

4 At this point, you should switch to the 3D Workspace (Photoshop will probably prompt you to do this). This highlights the **3D panel** and the **Properties panel**. Click and hold on the pop-up **Workspace** menu in the top right of the window, and drag down to select 3D

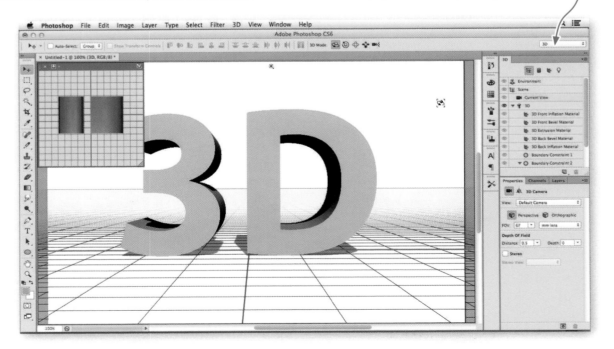

The Secondary View

AS THE NAME SUGGESTS, the Secondary View is there to give you an additional angle on your 3D scene. This is important because, unlike in standard Photoshop work, the third dimension means that you can't arrange several objects accurately using one view alone.

When you change to the 3D Workspace, the Secondary View appears in the top-left corner. You can choose between several different views of your object, and can swap the Main and Secondary views over with a single click. You can also hide it altogether, just bringing it into play when you need it. I've hidden the Secondary View in most of this book, as it often just gets in the way.

1 Here's the Secondary View as it first appears. It shows a top-down view of the scene, with the red and blue center lines matching those on the main view. This view is useful for arranging objects next to each other, so you can see how they interact.

The icon on the left shows the current view angle – top down, in this case ●

2 You can change the view by clicking on the icon that indicates the current view, and choosing a different one from the pop-up menu. When aligning several objects, you'll frequently want to check them from a number of angles ●

3 You can make the Secondary View bigger, if you wish, by dragging the marker in the bottom-right corner. There are two remaining icons:

● The **Close** icon puts the Secondary View away (you can find it again using **View > Show > 3D Secondary View**.

The **Swap** icon swaps the Secondary View with the main view ●

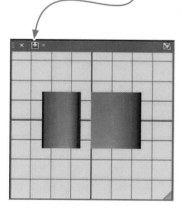

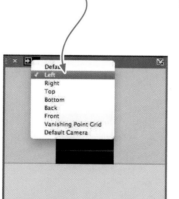

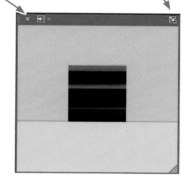

4 The bottom three views are of particular interest, since they show the scene in different ways:

● The **Front** view (left) displays the scene head-on, as would be expected, but without any perspective.

● The **Default Camera** (right) also shows a front view, but this time with perspective so it looks more like a 3D scene.

● The **Vanishing Point Grid** is a special case, which we'll look at later in the book.

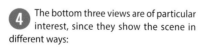

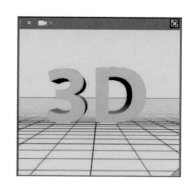

Moving the 3D world

WHEN YOU'RE WORKING IN 3D, the objects you create are separate from the world in which you create them. Very often we'll want to rotate our *view* of an object, so we can see it from a variety of angles, without rotating the object itself. We'll start by looking at the controls for moving our world view.

When working on a layer that contains 3D objects, the Move tool changes its function, and becomes the tool with which we manipulate the 3D environment. The Options Bar displays the tools that allow us to move around in the space in different ways. You can access the Move tool by pressing V on your keyboard.

> To move the world, make sure the object itself is not selected. If you see a rectangular bounding box around it, click anywhere on the canvas away from it to deselect the object.

1 The **Rotate tool** allows you to spin the view around freely – try it with the extruded 3D text you just created.

As you turn the view, you'll notice that the object doesn't move off the **Ground Plane** (the grid floor on which it sits).

You'll also notice that the shadows stay in the same place relative to the ground. That's because when you rotate the world view in this way, you're rotating all the lighting along with it.

2 The **Roll tool** turns the view on a flat plane parallel with your monitor. This is useful when you want to arrange the view so that all the verticals point straight up and down, for instance.

You can access the **Roll tool** temporarily when the **Rotate tool** is selected, by holding ⌥ *alt* on your keyboard.

 Keyboard shortcuts   MAC WIN BOTH

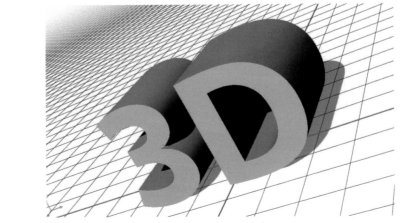

3 The **Drag tool** moves the 3D scene around without rotating it. This is the result of dragging the original setup, as seen in step 1, to the right.

The view will move in perspective as you drag it, but you won't move around it: this tool only drags left to right, up and down.

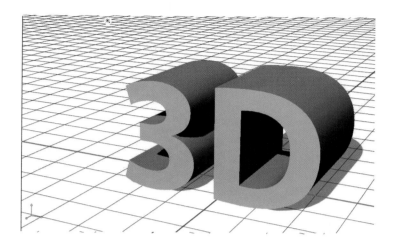

4 The **Slide tool** slides the view back and forth in 3D space. Where the **Drag tool** moves the object in the plane of your monitor, the **Slide tool** moves it perpendicular to your monitor.

It's particularly useful for zooming in to see the fine detail of a scene, or zooming out to see the whole thing.

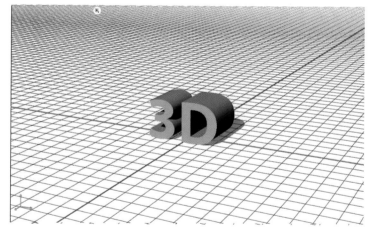

5 The **Scale tool** makes the scene larger and smaller. When working with no 3D object selected, as we are here, it behaves in a similar way to the **Slide tool**; but when we've selected an object, it will scale just that item independently of the scene or of other objects in the scene.

Note that this icon will change when an object is selected, to show object scaling rather than camera movement.

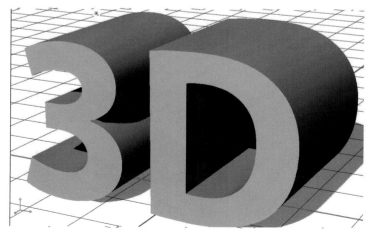

Moving 3D objects around

MOVING OBJECTS AROUND is a different process from moving your view of the object. When an object is selected, the Move tool will move just that object, leaving the rest of the world alone.

Photoshop uses a variety of methods for dragging, sliding, rotating and scaling 3D objects, and they quickly become intuitive after just a couple of minutes' use. The key to performing each action successfully is to study the explanatory text that appears as you move the cursor around – the so-called Head-Up Display that means you can see what you're doing without taking your eyes off the focus of interest.

Even with tools as easy to use as these, you can still make mistakes. Remember, you can always use the Undo command (⌘ Z *ctrl* Z) to reverse the last action, as well as Multiple Undo (⌘ ⌥ Z *ctrl* *alt* Z) to step backward through the last 20 or so actions.

① As you move the cursor over a 3D object, a bounding box will appear around it to show it has been selected.

Click on an object to select it. The box will turn pale yellow to indicate it has been selected, and an axis indicator will appear in the middle of the box (as seen in the following screen shots).

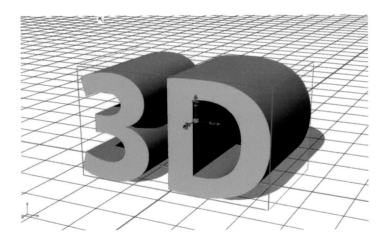

② As you move the cursor over each face of the object, that face will highlight, and will appear in a slightly deeper shade of yellow.

Click and drag on any face to slide the object along in a plane perpendicular to that face. As you move over each face, edge and corner, explanatory text will appear showing you what will happen if you drag the object.

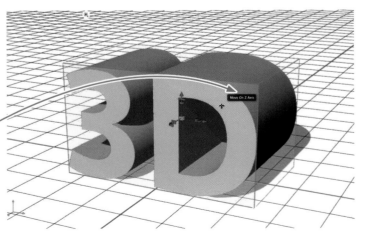

Move On Z Axis

Keyboard shortcuts　　MAC WIN BOTH

3 When you move the cursor over the front face, the words *Move Along Z* appear, as seen below. Dragging on this face will slide the object back and forth on this axis, but will not move it side to side.

The pop-up text that explained how the **Move tool** works is now replaced by information showing the distance dragged.

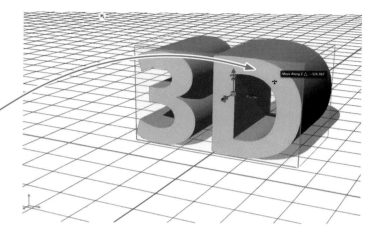

4 As well as moving on the Z axis, you can of course move on the X and Y axes by dragging on the appropriate sides.

If you move the cursor *over an edge*, you'll be able to drag the object in the plane perpendicular to that edge. So here, by dragging on the vertical Y-axis edge, we can move on the XZ plane.

This is equivalent to moving on both the X and Z axes simultaneously.

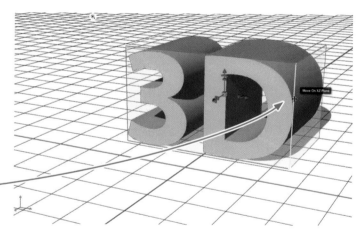

5 Dragging an object on the XZ plane means moving it on the **Ground Plane**, and that's an especially useful thing to be able to do.

Once again, as you drag the readout will show the exact distance you've moved the object, in both dimensions.

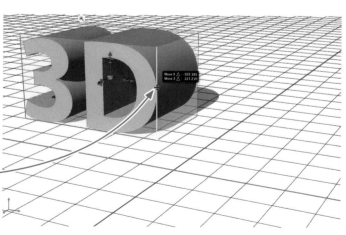

Rotating 3D objects

1 When you move the cursor *over* an edge, you can drag the object on the plane perpendicular to that edge, as we've seen. But when you move it *near* to the edge, the **Move tool** will rotate the object around the axis parallel to that edge.

As before, pop-up help text explains exactly what's going to happen to the object when you click and drag.

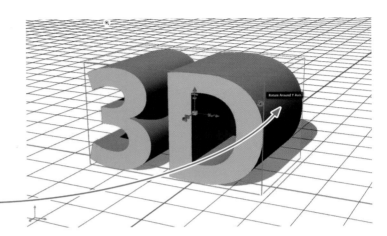

2 As you start to drag, the text changes to show the precise angle of rotation, as well displaying as the axis that you're rotating around.

It takes a little practice to gauge whether you're going to slide or rotate an axis, as the controls are very close to each other; but the explanatory text will always help to show what's going to happen.

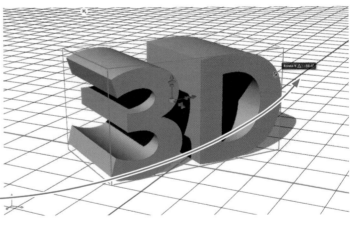

3 You can also freely rotate the object by positioning the cursor anywhere outside its bounding box, while it's still selected. The **Move tool** now behaves much more as it does when rotating the entire scene; you're simply spinning the object around in space.

When you rotate the object in this way, there's no explanatory text to show the multiple angles of rotation.

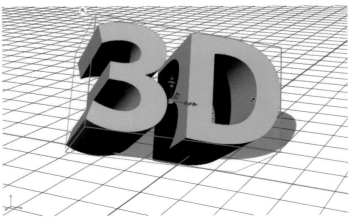

Moving using the 3D axis

WE'VE LOOKED AT MOVING OBJECTS by dragging directly on them, using the Head-Up Display approach to movement and rotation. But there are times when you can't access the control you need: for example, if you're looking at an object head-on, then you can't reach either side in order to slide it sideways along the ground plane.

The 3D axis was the method of moving objects before Photoshop CS6 brought in the new approach. It's still there, and is a useful alternative. To use it, move your cursor over any of the elements of the controller, and that element will highlight in yellow to show it's the active control.

1 At the end of each axis arm is the **Move** control, shown as a cone. Clicking and dragging on this will move the object along that axis. Drag in the direction you want the object to move.

As you drag, a readout shows the axis you're moving along, and the direction moved.

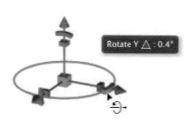

2 The **Rotation** controls appear just below the Move controls, and are shown as a tiny arc segment. As you move over one, it will spring into a full circle, and you can drag to rotate the object around the axis perpendicular to that circle.

Once again, the readout shows the angle of rotation.

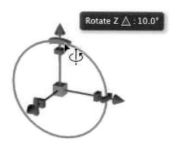

3 The **Scale** controls are just below the Rotation control, and allow you to scale an object along just one axis at a time.

In the center of the **3D Axis** is the **Uniform Scale** control, and dragging on this will scale the entire object (right).

As before, the readout shows the scale amount.

Getting back to where you started

WHEN YOU MOVE OBJECTS AROUND it's easy to lose track of their orientation, and when you come to combine multiple objects this can cause problems.

The Properties panel is the key to understanding everything about an object's size, position and rotation – as well as just about every facet of its appearance. We'll look at the Properties panel in much more detail later in the book. For now, we'll concentrate on how we can use it to correct an awkward positioning.

1 The **Properties panel** should be on view when you switch to the **3D workspace**. If it isn't, choose it from the **Window** menu. This is how the panel looks when an object is selected. It shows basic information about the object, such as the extrusion depth, text color, and so on.

At the top are four buttons that switch between different sets of information. This default view is the **Mesh** pane. You can switch between different panes by clicking on these icons ●

2 To reset an object's position, click on the final icon, which reveals the **Coordinates** pane. The name of the pane appears to the right of the icons.

This pane displays three columns, showing:

● The object's position in space

● The object's angle of rotation

● The object's scale.

If you've changed any of these settings, the altered values will be shown here ●

3 If you only want to place an object back on the **Ground Plane**, then select the X field and type 0 into it; press ➡ to go to the Y field, and type 0 again; then press ➡ to go to the Z field and type 0 a third time.

Alternatively, you can click the **Reset Coordinates** button at the bottom. This will reset not only the object's angles of rotation, but its position and scale ●

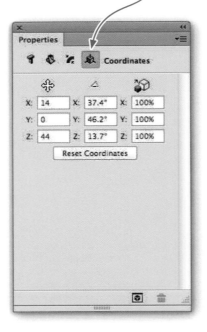

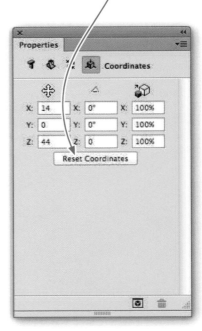

If your **Properties panel** doesn't show the **Mesh** pane, but instead shows a **Materials** pane, then click on the object once more with the **Move tool** to reset it. If it instead shows the **3D Camera** view, then you don't have the object selected – this is displaying world settings instead. Click on your object to select it.

2 Shaping and editing a 3D object

SO FAR WE'VE LOOKED at moving an object around in 3D space. In this chapter, we'll see how we can change the shape of that object, by extruding, twisting and tapering it. We'll work with the same basic text object we created on page 7.

To make the images here clearer and less cluttered, I've hidden the Ground Plane and the Secondary View, and stripped away the window frame so only the object remains on view.

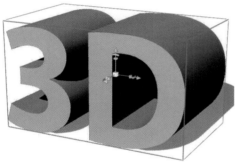

1 Here's the object as we left it at the end of the last chapter. It's selected, and you can see the 3D axis indicator in the middle.

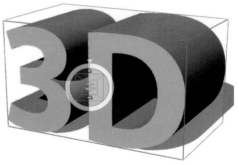

2 With the object still selected, press **V** on your keyboard, and a new set of Head-Up Display controls appears in the center.

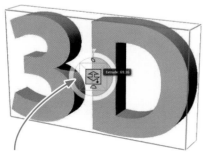

3 In the middle of the ring you'll find the **Extrude** control. Click and drag downward on this to make the object less deep. Note how the explanatory text shows the extrusion depth.

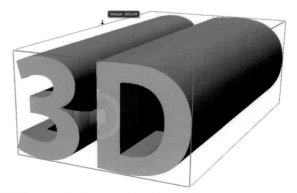

4 You can also drag upward on the **Extrude** control to make the object deeper, of course. Once again, the explanatory text shows how deep the object is.

Tapering, bending and twisting

EXTRUDING IS THE MOST COMMON method of adapting a 3D object, but it isn't the only one. There are three more methods we can use to distort the object using this first batch of controls: we can taper it, bend it, and twist it (and in the following chapters we'll look at rotation, inflation and bevels as well). All the controls are accessed using the Head-Up Display icons that appear in the middle of the object. Dragging on different areas of this controller will produce different results.

In these examples, I've used Undo after each step to reset the object to its original shape, so that each action is carried out on the basic 3D object.

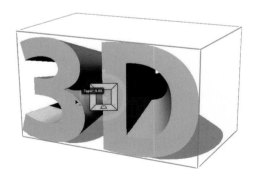

1 This is the way the object looks when you first click on it. In order to access the distortion controls, you need to press **V** on your keyboard each time you select it.

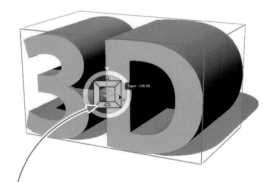

2 On the previous page we looked at the **Extrude** control, right in the middle. Around this is a four-sided box that highlights as you roll over it: this is the **Taper** control.

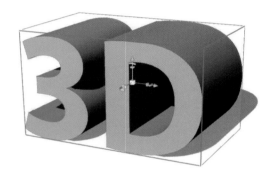

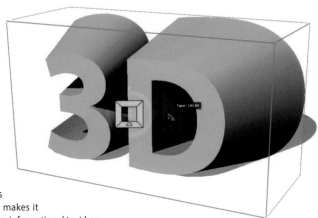

3 Tapering an object makes it become larger or smaller as it recedes away from you. Clicking on this control and dragging to the left makes it smaller (above); dragging to the right will make it larger (right). As usual, an informational text box appears as you drag to display the amount of the taper.

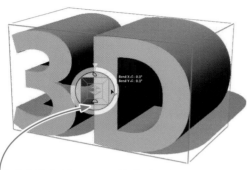

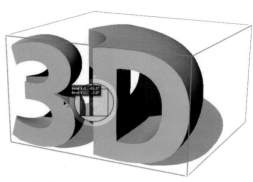

4 Outside the **Taper** control is the **Bend** control, which is formed of four small circle segments. Unlike the previous two controls, this can be dragged in any direction.

5 Dragging to the left will, as you'd expect, bend the object to the left. But you'll also have difficulty not bending it up and down to a small degree as well—we'll see how to deal with that overleaf.

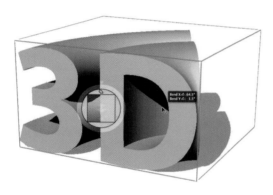

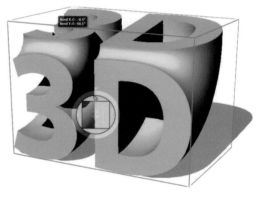

6 Dragging to the right bends the object in that direction. Once again, the pop-up information shows the bend amount.

7 You can also drag the object up and down to bend it vertically—or a combination of the two to bend it in any direction.

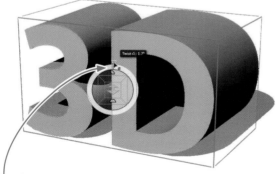

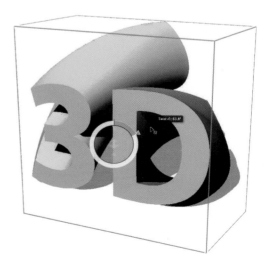

8 The outer ring on the Head-Up Display holds the **Twist** control. This is a rotary dial that twists the object around an axis perpendicular to the front face—in other words, around the Z axis.

Distorting in combination

WE'VE LOOKED AT EACH DISTORTION individually, but of course they can be combined to produce complex forms. All the distortion information is stored within the 3D object, so you're never committed to a particular effect; you can always go back and change it later.

1 Let's start by using the **Bend** control to twist this object to the right. As you can see, it has started to intersect itself, which produces an ungainly result.

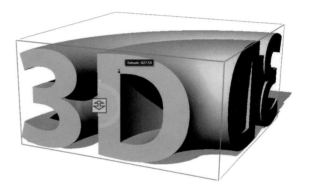

2 We can fix this by using the **Extrude** control to make the object deeper. Now, a much longer object is being bent around itself, so it forms a much smoother curve.

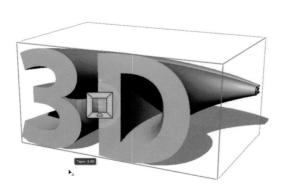

3 We can add some **Taper** to the mix, so the object gets smaller as it recedes into the distance. It's still bent to the right, though, and forms this interesting shape.

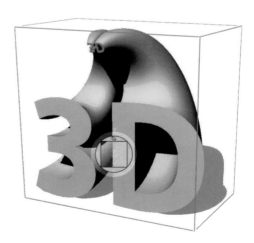

4 Even though we'd bent it to the right in the first step, we can change that if we like, simply by dragging on the **Bend** control. Now, it's bent up on itself, appearing tiny and upside down in the air.

Distortion with numerical accuracy

DRAGGING ON THE HEAD-UP DISPLAY controller is all very well, but it's difficult to make accurate distortions that way. It's much better to start sketching out the shape you want by dragging the controller, and then refine it using the Properties panel.

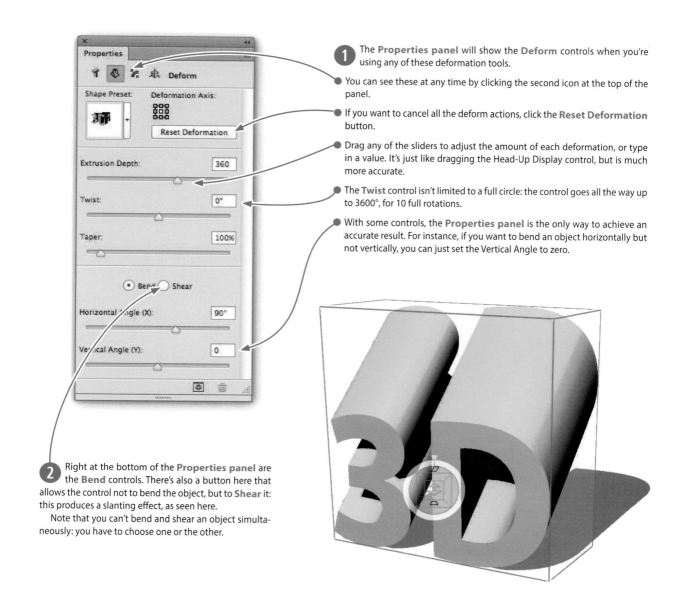

1 The **Properties panel** will show the **Deform** controls when you're using any of these deformation tools.

● You can see these at any time by clicking the second icon at the top of the panel.

● If you want to cancel all the deform actions, click the **Reset Deformation** button.

● Drag any of the sliders to adjust the amount of each deformation, or type in a value. It's just like dragging the Head-Up Display control, but is much more accurate.

● The **Twist** control isn't limited to a full circle: the control goes all the way up to 3600°, for 10 full rotations.

● With some controls, the **Properties panel** is the only way to achieve an accurate result. For instance, if you want to bend an object horizontally but not vertically, you can just set the Vertical Angle to zero.

2 Right at the bottom of the **Properties panel** are the **Bend** controls. There's also a button here that allows the control not to bend the object, but to **Shear** it: this produces a slanting effect, as seen here.

Note that you can't bend and shear an object simultaneously: you have to choose one or the other.

If the cap fits...

THE DISTORTIONS WE'VE APPLIED so far in this chapter have all been to do with deforming the *sides* of the extruded object. The next set of controls set the behavior of the *cap* of the object.

There are two sets of controls: Bevel and Inflate. We'll look at each in turn. There's a lot more to the Inflate control than is covered in this introduction: see Chapter 5 for a more detailed look.

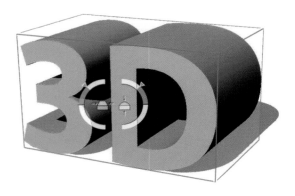

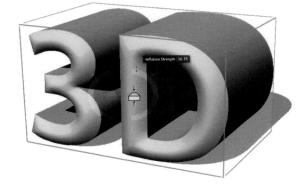

1 When you click on the object with the **Move tool** it becomes selected; press **V** and the **Extrude** controls appear. Press **V** a second time to reveal the controls for the cap.

2 On the right are the **Inflate** controls. Click and drag up on this to blow out the front of the object, and it will appear as if it were inflated with air.

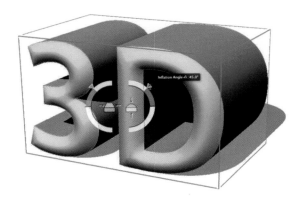

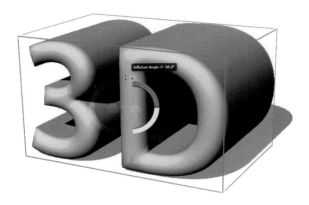

3 Outside each control is a radial angle control, which sets the angle between the effect and the face of the object. The default angle is 45°; drag up and down to change this angle.

4 Here's the result of dragging the Inflation Angle up to its maximum value of 90°. You can see how the face now appears to inflate directly out of the sides, with no hard line between the two.

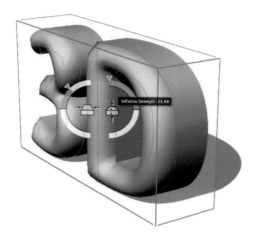

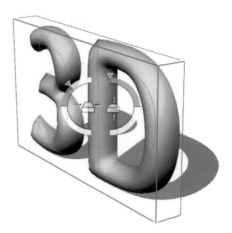

5 When we turn the object to view it from the side, we can see that only the front face has been inflated. That's the default setting – the back of the object remains perfectly flat.

6 We can see this more clearly if we reduce the **Extrusion** setting to zero. This is easily done using the **Properties panel**, on the **Deform** pane.

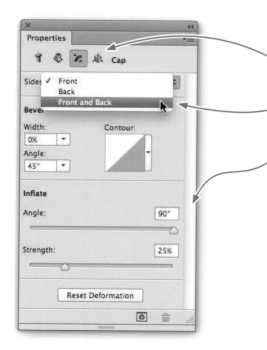

7 When you select the **Cap** pane, the **Properties panel** changes to display the third set of controls.

● You can also access this by clicking on the third button at the top of the panel.

● Click on the word **Front** in the pop-up menu labeled **Sides**, and this menu will appear: choose **Front and Back** to apply the inflation to both faces of the object (see below).

● As usual, you can also change the angle and strength of the inflation by dragging the sliders, or by typing in values numerically.

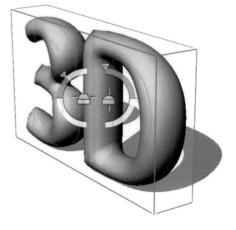

Turning on the bevel

WHERE INFLATION PRODUCES a smooth, bulbous cap, adding a Bevel instead adds a hard, chamfered edge between the face (the cap) and the side of the object. You can also choose from a variety of built-in bevel shapes, or you can draw your own.

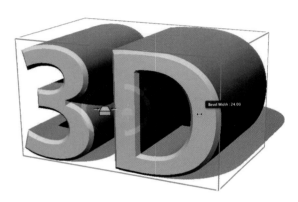

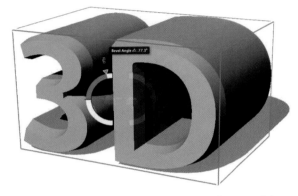

1 Click and drag on the icon in the left half of the Head-Up Display to add a **Bevel** to the object. The more you drag, the stronger the bevel will be.

2 As with the **Inflate** control, you can drag on the rotary dial to set the Bevel angle. The maximum value is 85° – if it were 90°, the bevel would be (literally) infinitely large.

3 The default is a flat bevel, but you can choose a shape. Click on the down-pointing arrow next to the **Contour** thumbnail to open the picker, and choose a shape to see that shape on the object.

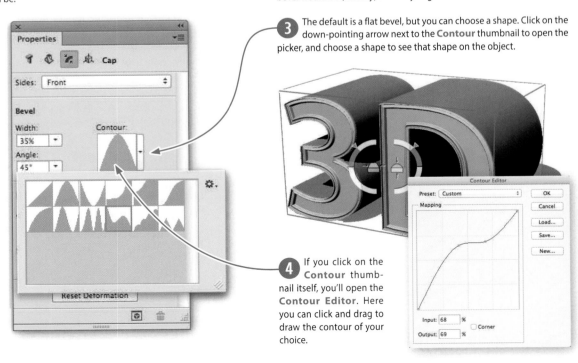

4 If you click on the **Contour** thumbnail itself, you'll open the **Contour Editor**. Here you can click and drag to draw the contour of your choice.

Editing the source

EVEN THOUGH we've extruded, bent, twisted, bevelled and inflated our text, we can still edit its basic appearance. This is one of the most surprising things about working with 3D objects in Photoshop: everything remains editable, at all times.

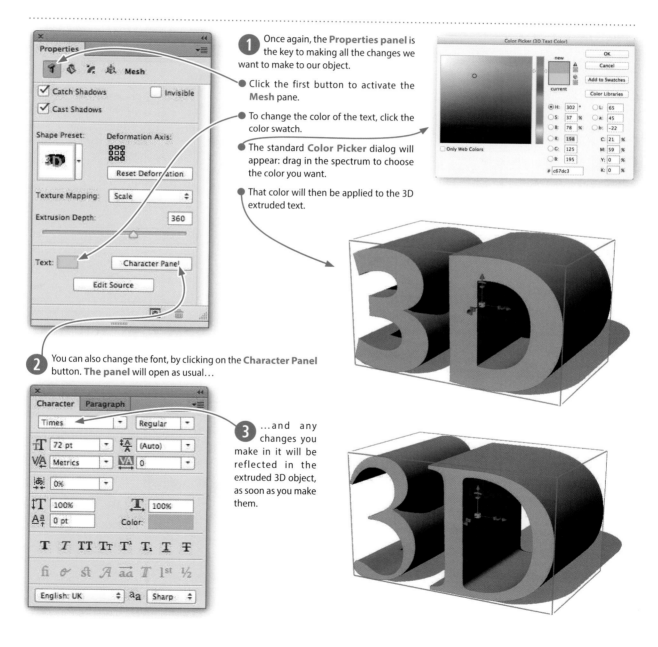

1 Once again, the **Properties panel** is the key to making all the changes we want to make to our object.

● Click the first button to activate the **Mesh** pane.

● To change the color of the text, click the color swatch.

● The standard **Color Picker** dialog will appear: drag in the spectrum to choose the color you want.

● That color will then be applied to the 3D extruded text.

2 You can also change the font, by clicking on the **Character Panel** button. **The panel** will open as usual…

3 …and any changes you make in it will be reflected in the extruded 3D object, as soon as you make them.

Editing the contents

WE'VE SEEN HOW you can change the font and color of type – now, here's how you can change the text itself, even after you've applied all the 3D effects to it.

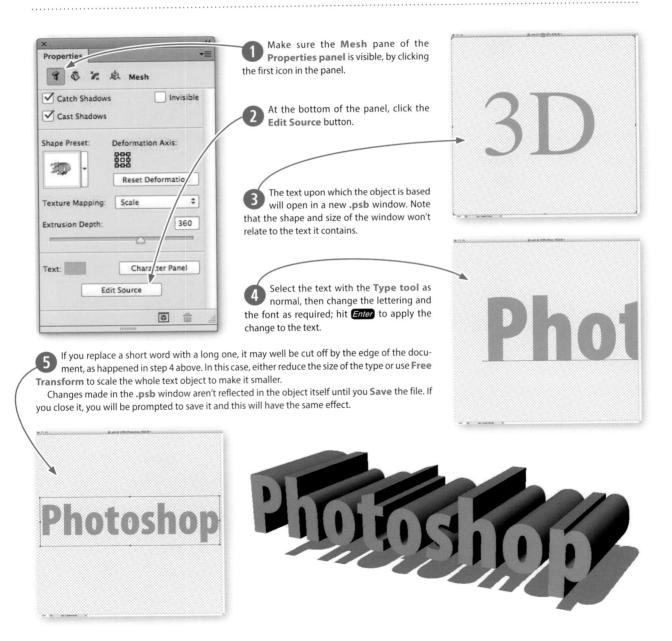

1 Make sure the **Mesh** pane of the **Properties panel** is visible, by clicking the first icon in the panel.

2 At the bottom of the panel, click the **Edit Source** button.

3 The text upon which the object is based will open in a new **.psb** window. Note that the shape and size of the window won't relate to the text it contains.

4 Select the text with the **Type tool** as normal, then change the lettering and the font as required; hit *Enter* to apply the change to the text.

5 If you replace a short word with a long one, it may well be cut off by the edge of the document, as happened in step 4 above. In this case, either reduce the size of the type or use **Free Transform** to scale the whole text object to make it smaller.

Changes made in the **.psb** window aren't reflected in the object itself until you **Save** the file. If you close it, you will be prompted to save it and this will have the same effect.

3 Revolving a 3D object

IN THE PREVIOUS CHAPTER we looked briefly at using the Bend control to twist an extruded object around either the X or Y axis. But that's only a small part of the capability of this control: it's capable of much more dramatic results.

The Bend control can also be used to revolve an object as if it were on a lathe, or on a potter's wheel. This gives us the freedom to design bottles, glasses, vases, spears, and just about any other object that has a rotational symmetry.

Where we used the Type tool to create our starting object previously, here we'll see how Photoshop can create 3D objects from just about any source. We'll begin by drawing a simple outline with the Brush tool, which we'll then turn into a bottle.

1 Start by making a new layer. Switch to the **Brush tool** and choose a small, hard-edged brush.

With a mid-gray as the foreground color, sketch out a shape. I've gone for a gourd-like bottle shape, but you can choose to paint any shape you like.

2 In the **3D panel**, set the **Source** to **Selected Layer(s)**, and check the **3D Extrusion** radio button. Then hit the **Create** button.

3 Here's what you'll get. The default method for turning a layer into a shape is to extrude it along the **Z axis** a little way. You can see how it casts a shadow on the **Ground Plane**.

Turning the extrusion into a revolve

AT THIS POINT, you may be wondering why the shape has been extruded rather than revolved. That's because we haven't changed the settings yet: a straightforward, linear extrusion along the Z-axis is the default Photoshop behavior.

On these pages we'll see how to remove that extrusion entirely, and replace it with a fully rounded Bend operation that turns the drawn outline into a solid, filled shape.

1 Click on the 3D object with the **Move tool**, and you'll see the familiar bounding box that displays the 3D axis controller in the middle.

2 Press the **V** key on your keyboard, and the first batch of **Head-Up Controls** will appear.

3 You could adjust the extrusion and rotation using the HUD controls, as explained in the previous chapter, but that's an inaccurate and unnecessarily clumsy way to do it.

A much better approach is to open the **Properties panel**, which should now be displaying the **Deform** pane (if it isn't, choose the second button from the left at the top of the panel).

Set the **Extrusion Depth** to zero to remove the extrusion altogether from the 3D object.

4 With no extrusion at all, the object now appears as a flat shape, very similar to the one we first drew.

Only the existence of the shadow gives away the fact that it's a 3D object.

5 With the extrusion removed, we can now revolve the object. Dragging the **Bend** control directly on the object can affect both the X and Y angles simultaneously; it's hard to control just one and not the other with that method.

Instead, drag the **Horizontal Angle** control at the bottom of the **Properties panel** to its maximum value of 360°. This is a full circle rotation

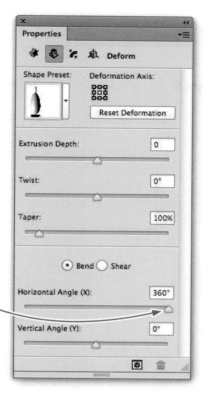

6 The more eagle-eyed among you will have spotted that the object above doesn't look quite as you expected.

That's because it has been revolved around its *center*. Since we drew the left side of the bottle, we want it to revolve around its *right side*.

The axis about which an object is revolved is called the **Deformation Axis**, and it's controlled by the small icon at the top of the **Properties panel**. By default, the axis is set to the center; click on the middle point on the right of the axis to change it

On the right is the result of clicking that button. With the axis moved to the right, the bottle has been duly rotated around that side.

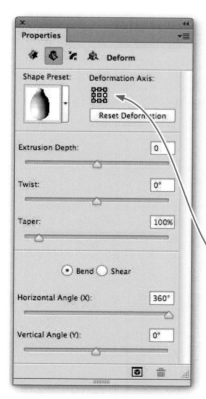

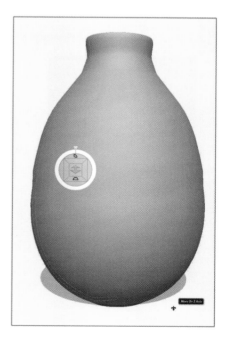

Using the Pen tool for more control

IF YOU FOLLOWED the tutorial in the first three pages of this chapter, you'll have realized that while it's perfectly possible to create a 3D object from an outline drawn with the Brush tool, the outcome is far from satisfactory. The tool is hard to control with any accuracy, it's very difficult to draw a smooth line with it, and it's almost impossible to get rid of the lumps and wrinkles afterwards.

A far better solution is to use the Pen tool, which is the best way to produce smooth curves. It also makes it much easier to edit the drawn shapes after it has been revolved, as we'll see later in the chapter. The only problem with it is that the Pen tool is notorious for being the hardest Photoshop tool to master. All I can do is suggest you take the time to learn how to use it – especially if you're going to be working in Photoshop's 3D environment to any great extent.

1 Start by making a new document, then make a new layer within that document. Make sure the **Pen tool** is set to create **Paths** rather than **Shapes** – you set this using the pop-up menu on the far left of the tool's **Options Bar**.

Draw the outline of your object, as if it had been sliced through the middle and you were looking at a cross section. I've drawn the profile of a wine glass.

2 Close the path by joining the start and end points, as above. Otherwise, you'll get a warning message like this:

3 With the path drawn, set the **Source** as **Work Path**, and check the **3D Extrusion** radio button. Then hit the **Create** button to continue. The result is the path extruded along the Z-axis, just as you'd expect it to be.

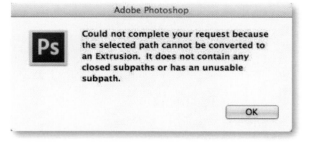

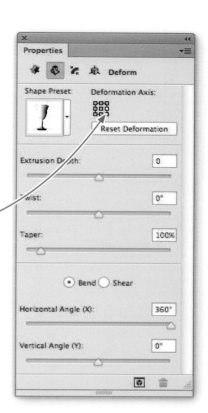

4 We now need to change that extrusion into a revolve operation, using the technique described on the previous spread: set the **Extrusion Depth** to zero, and the **Horizontal Angle** to 360°.

Once again, the default is for the object to be revolved around its center. Note the smooth, cylindrical sides, which are a result of revolving that hard right edge (which forms the center of the stem) around the middle of the object.

5 Changing the **Deformation Axis** from the center of the object to the right edge now revolves it around that axis.

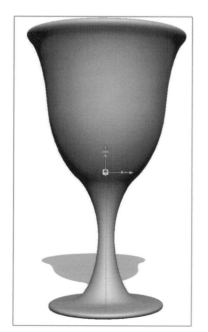

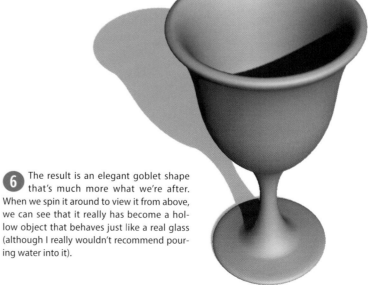

6 The result is an elegant goblet shape that's much more what we're after. When we spin it around to view it from above, we can see that it really has become a hollow object that behaves just like a real glass (although I really wouldn't recommend pouring water into it).

Reshaping revolved shapes

JUST AS WE CAN EDIT extruded text, so we can edit a path to change the shape of the object extruded from it. This gives us tremendous flexibility, as it means we don't have to get the shape right first time.

First, though, we'll see what happens when we modify the deformation applied to an object, using just the Properties panel to change the parameters.

1 To create a lathed object that exactly matched the profile, we reduced the **Extrusion Depth** to zero.

If we now increase that extrusion amount, the effect is to move the axis of rotation so it's offset by that figure.

Here, for instance, increasing the depth to 400 makes the goblet much fatter, giving it a thicker stem (right)●

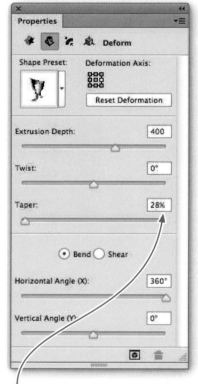

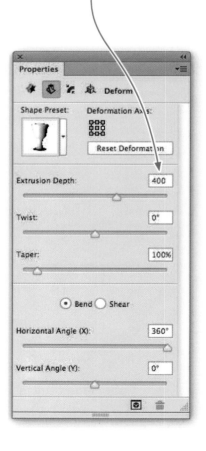

2 We can bring in all the other deformation controls, as well, which will affect the look of the object in interesting and often bizarre ways.

The default value for the **Taper** slider is 100%, which is no tapering at all (since the deformation can both increase and decrease the tapering of the object).

Here, reducing the taper amount to just 28% causes the object to fold in on itself, producing this curious result (left). It may no longer be a wine goblet, but it's certainly a novel shape.

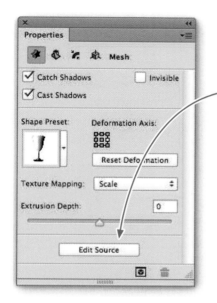

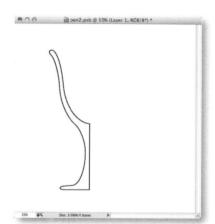

3 Now let's look at reshaping the outline. In the **Properties panel**, click the first button at the top so that the **Mesh** pane is visible. At the bottom of the panel, click the **Edit Source** button.

The path will open in a new **.psb** window – the internal file format used by Photoshop for storing objects inside one another. (You'll see a standard checkerboard background behind your path; I've added a white background here to make the path easier to see in print.)

If you have Photoshop set to open new documents as Tabs, then detach this window from the tab set by dragging it out, so you can see it and the 3D object at the same time.

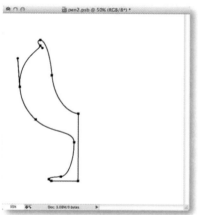

4 You can make any changes you like to the shape of the path, moving points around and changing their position and angle. Every time you **Save** the **.psb** document, the changes you've made will be reflected in the 3D object.

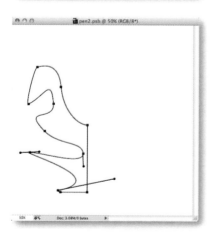

5 You don't, of course, have to stick within the bounds of drawing a plausible goblet – or even a feasible 3D object. However you distort the path, the changes will take immediate effect each time you **Save** the file.

When you've finished, you can simply **Close** the **.psb** file.

Refining the shape

THE ABILITY TO EDIT SHAPES means much more than just correcting our mistakes: we can create a 3D model interactively, watching how each correction affects the shape of the finished object. Here, we'll look at how we can use this technique to create a model of a wine bottle.

1 Start by sketching out a shape with the **Pen tool**, then use the technique described throughout this chapter to turn it into a revolved 3D object. You can see how this bottle is squat and ugly. At this stage, I haven't bothered with the inside: it's just a solid block.

2 Clicking the **Edit Source** button in the **Mesh** section of the **Properties panel** lets us access the outline. Make minor adjustments to the path, using ⌘ S ctrl S to save the .psb file each time so you can see the results instantly.

3 Once you've got the exterior of the bottle the way you want it, place the points to build the inside. This is important because, in a later chapter, we're going to look at turning this bottle transparent.

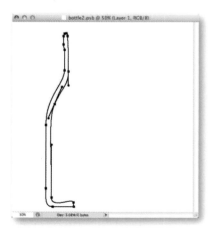

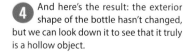

4 And here's the result: the exterior shape of the bottle hasn't changed, but we can look down it to see that it truly is a hollow object.

4 Inflating objects from photographs

AS WELL AS MODELING 3D objects from scratch, we can also create them directly from photographs, using Photoshop's inflation tool. This is the equivalent of pumping an object full of air, and it's a great way to turn flat artwork into dynamic models.

Not all photographs can be inflated – sometimes the technique just doesn't work, as we'll see at the end of the chapter. But when it does work, the results can be spectacular. In this chapter we'll begin with a simple cutout photograph of a beetle, and show what happens when we inflate it rather than extrude it.

I've hidden both the Ground Plane and the Secondary View, as usual, so we can concentrate on the object we're working on.

....

1 Here's our starting object: a top-down view of a beetle. It was photographed on a plain white background, and I've already removed that background using the **Magic Eraser tool**. You can download this beetle from **3DPhotoshop.net**.

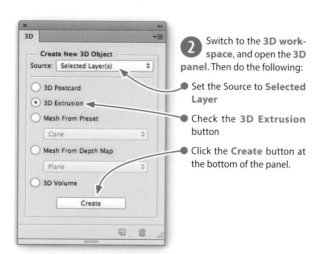

2 Switch to the **3D workspace**, and open the **3D panel**. Then do the following:

● Set the Source to **Selected Layer**

● Check the **3D Extrusion** button

● Click the **Create** button at the bottom of the panel.

3 Your beetle will be extruded as normal, and it will look like the image on the right. You can see here how it's been extruded into the distance.

4 When you turn the object around with the **Move tool**, you can see the result of the inflation procedure: it's been extended downward, and still has a flat top.

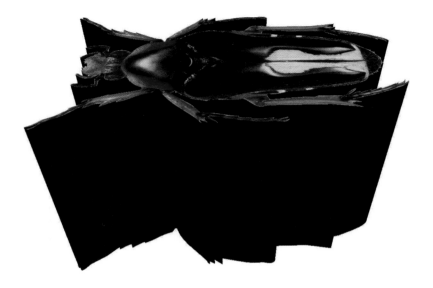

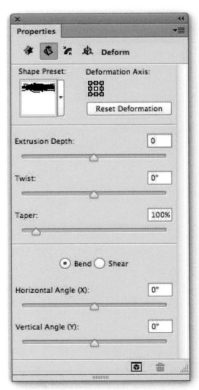

5 Select the object and press **V** on your keyboard to access the **Head-Up Display** in the middle. Drag the **Extrusion** control until the beetle has no depth.

When you drag the control, it's easy to set a negative extrusion amount by accident. A surer way of achieving the result is to use the **Properties panel** to set the extrusion depth to zero, by typing the value into the number field.

6 Press **V** once more, and the **Head-Up Display** will change to show the second set of controls. Begin by dragging the **Inflation Angle** slider all the way up to the top, so it shows a value of 90°. You won't see any change in the beetle just yet

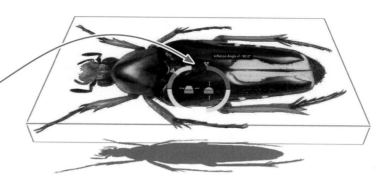

7 Now click on the **Inflate** control, and drag upward until your beetle is inflated as much as you think looks good. You can see that the body, being thicker, inflates much more than those thin legs – and that's exactly what we want

8 This is the result: a 3D beetle, generated in just a few seconds from that flat photograph, that you can spin around and view from any angle. It's really incredible that we're able to create this effect so easily, directly in Photoshop.

Save a preset

ONCE YOU'VE CREATED an object you like, you can save all the settings in a preset so you can retrieve them later. Here, we'll take all the settings for the beetle – zero extrusion, inflation angle set to 90°, and the inflation amount – and add that as a new preset.

Then, on the following page, we'll see how easy it is to apply the settings to a different object just by clicking on that preset.

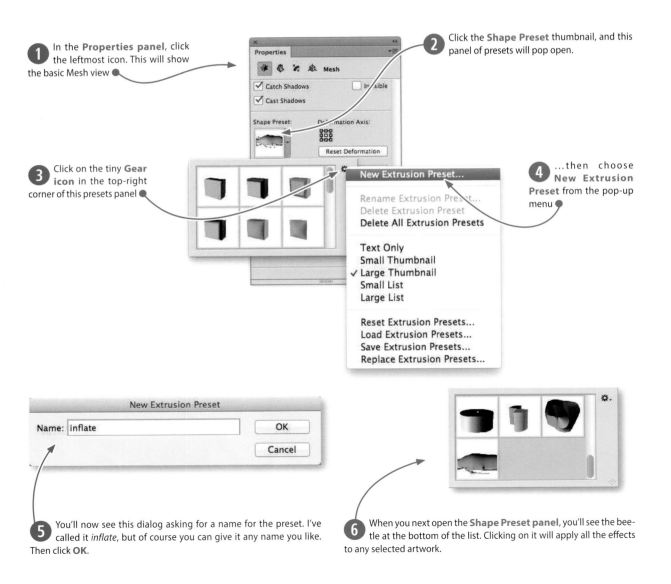

1 In the **Properties panel**, click the leftmost icon. This will show the basic Mesh view

2 Click the **Shape Preset** thumbnail, and this panel of presets will pop open.

3 Click on the tiny **Gear icon** in the top-right corner of this presets panel

4 ...then choose **New Extrusion Preset** from the pop-up menu

5 You'll now see this dialog asking for a name for the preset. I've called it *inflate*, but of course you can give it any name you like. Then click **OK**.

6 When you next open the **Shape Preset panel**, you'll see the beetle at the bottom of the list. Clicking on it will apply all the effects to any selected artwork.

Applying the preset

1 Here's our second photograph, a cutout of a larva. You can download it from **3DPhotoshop.net**.

2 Select the layer and choose **3D Extrusion from Layer** in the **3D panel**, then click **Create** to make the 3D object.

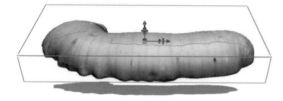

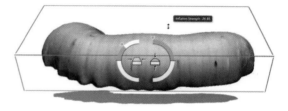

3 From the **Properties panel**, click on the first icon to go to the **Mesh** view and then choose the new preset, as described on the previous page.

4 Even though a preset has been applied, we can still modify the appearance. Here, I've dragged upward on the **Inflate** control to make the larva more rounded.

5 You'll end up with 3D models of both the beetle and the larva: when you place them into a scene, as I've done here, you can get some truly spectacular results.

Double-sided inflation

THE IMAGES WE INFLATED on the previous pages both ended up with flat bottoms, because that's more or less the way these objects are. But what of more rounded items, such as the pear in this photograph? We need a way to inflate this on both sides for a realistic view of the object.

Before we inflate it, though, let's look briefly at the best way to cut the image from its background.

1 This is the original photograph of the pear, and you can download it from **3DPhotoshop.net**.

2 Drag the **Quick Selection tool** over the *outside* of the pear to select the background. This is easier to select because it's so uniform.

3 Use **Select > Inverse** so that the pear is selected. Hold ⌥ _alt_ when dragging with the **Quick Selection tool** to subtract the shadow from the selection.

4 To clean up the selection, choose **Select > Refine Edge** or use the keyboard shortcut ⌘⌥R _ctrl_ _alt_ R. The background may appear as black, white or a checkerboard, depending on how you last set up the dialog.

PEAR PHOTO: DAREK POJDA ON WIKIMEDIA COMMONS

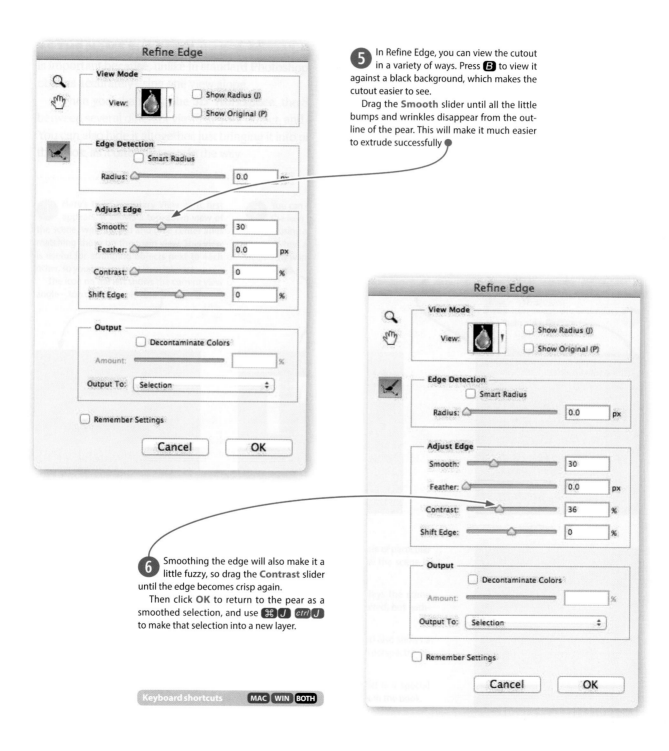

Refine Edge

View Mode

View:

☐ Show Radius (J)
☐ Show Original (P)

Edge Detection

☐ Smart Radius

Radius: △ 0.0

Adjust Edge

Smooth: 30

Feather: 0.0 px

Contrast: 0 %

Shift Edge: 0 %

Output

☐ Decontaminate Colors

Amount: %

Output To: Selection

☐ Remember Settings

Cancel   OK

5 In Refine Edge, you can view the cutout in a variety of ways. Press **B** to view it against a black background, which makes the cutout easier to see.

Drag the **Smooth** slider until all the little bumps and wrinkles disappear from the outline of the pear. This will make it much easier to extrude successfully ●

Refine Edge

View Mode

View:

☐ Show Radius (J)
☐ Show Original (P)

Edge Detection

☐ Smart Radius

Radius: △ 0.0 px

Adjust Edge

Smooth: △ 30

Feather: △ 0.0 px

Contrast: △ 36 %

Shift Edge: △ 0 %

Output

☐ Decontaminate Colors

Amount: %

Output To: Selection

☐ Remember Settings

Cancel   OK

6 Smoothing the edge will also make it a little fuzzy, so drag the **Contrast** slider until the edge becomes crisp again.

Then click **OK** to return to the pear as a smoothed selection, and use ⌘ **J** ctrl **J** to make that selection into a new layer.

Completing the effect

7 With the pear now cut away from its background, switch to the **3D panel** and extrude it as before, by choosing **3D Extrusion** and clicking the **Create** button.

You'll see the pear extruded backward, but it still has a flat face.

8 Select the first item in the **Properties panel**, to view the **Mesh** settings, and select the preset saved on page 38 to apply the beetle inflation effect to the pear.

You can see that the pear is now much more rounded on the front, but we're not finished yet.

9 When you use the **Move tool** to turn the pear around, you can see the problem: only half a pear is there. That's the issue we have to address next.

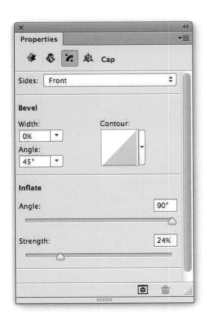

10 Take another look at the **Properties panel**, and switch to the **Cap** section by clicking the third icon at the top of the panel (this view will also appear when you use the **Inflate** controls).

Just below the top of the panel you'll see the **Sides** pop-up menu. This is currently set to **Front.**

11 Change this setting to **Front and Back**, to make the inflation effect apply to both sides of the object.

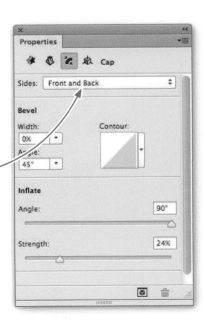

12 Changing the setting now gives a fully rounded pear, with the texture on both sides. What's actually happening here, though, is that the front texture is simply repeated on the back.

13 When you spin the pear around the inflation might seem too strong. You can adjust it, either by dragging directly on the **Head-Up Display** or by dragging the slider in the **Properties panel**.

14 Once again, in just a few clicks we're able to turn a flat photograph into a real 3D object that we can view from any angle. This gives us tremendous flexibility when working with such photographs.

Fixing the texture on the model

LOOKING AT THE PREVIOUS PAGES, you may have noticed an unsightly join line between the two halves of the pear. This is a common occurrence when a texture is mirrored. There's no perfect solution, but here are a few ways of getting rid of those imperfections.

1 You can see the join line clearly: it's an unsightly gray streak between the pear halves, and looks unnatural.

2 You could try the **Healing Brush** – but this samples dark areas that are then further shaded by the 3D rendering.

3 You can use the **Clone tool** directly on a 3D surface, sampling a nearby texture: this works in bright areas.

4 Where the **Clone tool** falls down is in dark areas, as it samples already shaded texture which is then shaded again.

5 A good option is to use the **Color Replacement tool**, nested in the **Brush tool** in the toolbar. Sample a color, then paint it over the gray line. It works fairly well in most cases ●

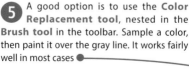

	Brush Tool	B
	Pencil Tool	B
■	Color Replacement Tool	B
	Mixer Brush Tool	B

Correcting highlights

6 There's some glare on this object, which comes from the lighting in the original photograph.

The problem is that glare will stay in the same place, even when the lighting on the object is from a completely different direction. Far better to get rid of it altogether.

7 To get rid of the glare, you need to address the texture that's wrapped around the object.

You can do this by looking at the **Layers panel**. In the **Textures** section, beneath the name of the 3D layer, you'll see the original texture listed (it may well be called Layer 1).

Double-click the layer thumbnail to open it in a new window

8 The texture is stored within the 3D object, and will open as a new **.psb** document. This is the internal file system that Photoshop uses for artwork that resides inside another layer.

9 Use the **Clone tool**, or you could try the **Healing Brush**, to paint out the shine – the choice is yours. It depends on the situation, as some tools will work better than others. The aim is to hide the shine altogether.

10 When you now **Save** the **.psb** document, the changes will be saved back into the texture that's wrapped around the pear (note that saving the .psb is *not* the same as saving the whole file). The glare has now gone, and the lighting is more realistic.

3D inflation from scratch

WE'VE LOOKED AT A COUPLE of different ways of inflating photographs, but – this being Photoshop, after all – we're not limited to just what we can capture with a camera. Any design can be turned into a 3D object, which means we can create the items we need without having to source images or models.

Here, we'll see how to draw a basic lifebelt, starting with nothing. It's not a complex model, but try finding a photograph of a lifebelt from the right angle and you'll see how hard it can be to track one down. It's so much easier to make an object that can be turned around at will.

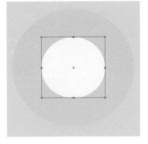

1 Start by making a new layer on a new document. Create a circular selection by holding **Shift** as you drag with the **Elliptical Marquee tool**.

2 Select a pale gray as the foreground color (white will be too bright), and press **⌥ Backspace** **alt Backspace** to fill the selection with that color.

3 Enter **QuickMask** mode (shortcut: **Q**): the selection appears in white on a red background. Use **⌘ T** **ctrl T** to enter **Free Transform** mode, then hold **⌥ Shift** **alt Shift** as you drag a corner handle toward the center, shrinking the circle.

4 Press **Q** again to leave **QuickMask** mode, then just hit **Backspace** to delete the new selection from the gray disc, leaving a donut shape.

5 Now for the color. Use the **Rectangular Marquee tool** to select the upper-right corner of the donut.

6 Select a bright red, and press **⌥ Shift Backspace** **alt Shift Backspace** to fill the selection with red (the **Shift** stops the color from leaking outside the existing pixels).

7 Make a similar selection in the bottom-left corner, and use the same method to fill that area with red as well.

8 Open the **3D panel** and use the usual method to extrude the lifebelt, turning it into a 3D object.

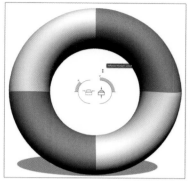

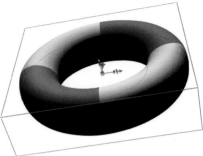

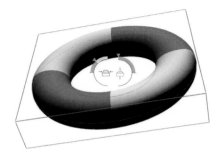

9 Use the preset created at the beginning of this chapter to turn that basic extruded shape into a rounded, three-dimensional lifebelt. When viewing it head-on, you can only guess at the inflation amount, but it's easy enough to fix this later.

10 Rotate the view so you can see the lifebelt from a side angle, and make the inflation double-sided by checking **Front and Back** in the **Mesh** section of the **Properties panel**, as we did before.

11 The lifebelt now looks a little too bulbous: in reality, they're flatter than that. So either use the Head-Up Display to make it thinner, or drag the **Strength** slider in the **Inflate** section of the **Properties panel** to make the inflation amount less extreme.

Here's how the lifebelt can appear when it's merged with other images to make a complete illustration.

If we wanted to make it more realistic it would be easy to add some more texture to the original design; or we could even start with a photograph of a real lifebelt.

Either way, the point is that it's easy to create exactly the object you need without having any source material at hand.

Objects you *can't* inflate

SO FAR IN THIS CHAPTER we've looked at a few success stories – photographs that naturally lend themselves to 3D inflation. But not all images are so fortunate; there's a lot of trial and error involved in finding pictures that will work using this technique.

Here, we'll look at a selection of objects that, theoretically, ought to be just right for inflation, but which, for different reasons, fail to produce convincing models.

1 This soccer ball, at first glance, may look as if it's the perfect object for this sort of treatment. After all, it's perfectly round, so surely that's the best shape for inflation?

The problem is that the regular pattern on it has already been photo-graphed wrapped around a sphere. When we then wrap it once more, it's blown out of proportion.

In addition, there's a significant problem at the seams, where the mirrored joins look des-perately unconvincing.
Verdict: **FAIL**.

2 This bottle should inflate perfectly: the thin neck will expand less than the wide body, after all. But look what happens: the base is blown out like a balloon. Verdict: **FAIL**.

3 Animals can work well, as we saw with the beetle and its larva. So how about extruding our four-legged friend?

4 At first glance, this seems to work fairly well. There's a slight problem with the back legs, though.

5 The real problem comes when we rotate it: it turns into a hideous, misshapen mutant monster. Verdict: **FAIL**.

5 3D postcards

COMPARED TO THE METHODS we've looked at so far for creating 3D objects, the 3D Postcard option is distinctly underpowered. It was an earlier, quick-fire method of turning an object into simple 3D, and it appeared in Photoshop long before the extrusion tools we've been looking at.

But 3D Postcards are a valid way of building quick, effective objects — and if you create them using a Smart Object as your starting point, you'll find that you can edit the contents easily.

1 You can use any artwork as the basis of a 3D Postcard. In homage to the name, though, let's start by building a real postcard in such a way that we can change all the elements later if we wish.

This postcard consists of just three layers: the background shot of the building with the palm trees, the *Greetings From* text, and the *Paradise* text.

You can download this complete postcard from **3DPhotoshop.net** if you wish.

2 Select all the layers, by holding the *Shift* key as you click on each one in the **Layers panel** (left).

3 Now choose **Layer > Smart Objects > Convert to Smart Object**, and you'll see that all those layers are replaced by a single icon (right).

Although it looks like it's all now just one layer, it actually contains all the layers from the document, as we'll see later.

Manipulating the postcard

4 In the **3D panel**, set the source to **Selected Layer(s)** and make sure the **3D Postcard** button is checked (*not* the 3D Extrusion button we've been using so far).

All you have to do now is hit the **Create** button to build the postcard.

5 When you first build the postcard you won't see any difference. But when you drag outside it with the **Move tool**, you'll see that it has been turned into a flat, 3D object that can be spun around and viewed from any angle.

Although the object is flat, it will be contained within a bounding box that has some depth to it. This is to make it easier to manipulate the object using the **Head-Up Controls** as detailed on page 12.

6 It can be very hard to reach the edges of a 3D postcard when you want to move it around. In this instance, it's much better to use the **3D axis**, as explained on page 15. Click on the 3D object and the axis will appear in the middle.

The first thing you'll want to do is to reduce the size of the postcard, using the box at the junction of the three axis indicators. That's because creating a 3D postcard from an image will always build it at the size of the image, which gives you no wiggle room.

7 As you turn the postcard around, you can see that it really does behave like a real postcard – until you spin it to view the back, that is. Instead of space for an address and a message there's a reversed version of the image on the front.

You can't do anything about this; 3D postcards in Photoshop are single-sided objects, and you can't define a different texture for the reverse side.

8 Let's see how we can change the appearance of the postcard. Look in the **Layers panel**, and you'll see the textures listed below the name of the layer. Right at the bottom is the word *Paradise*; that's the name of the Smart Object layer (when you make a Smart Object, it always takes the name of the uppermost layer in the selection).

Double-click that *Paradise* layer and the texture will open in a new window.

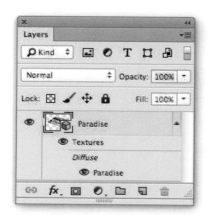

9 When the texture opens, it will appear in a new window and it will have this grid overlay on top of it. When you now look at the **Layers panel**, you'll see it looks just like the panel did immediately after we created the Smart Object (see step 2).

Double-click the **Smart Object** layer, which will also be named *Paradise*, in this new **Layers panel**, and once again it will open in a new window.

Editing the Smart Object

10 Double-clicking a **Smart Object** opens it in a new window – and now you'll see how all those original layers remain intact. You can edit all the text if you like, or just change the Layer Effects to different colors. You could even replace the background picture with a completely different one.

11 Here's how the postcard looks after making a couple of minor changes – changing the word *Paradise* to *Egypt*, which is where I took the photograph; and adjusting the colors to make the fill and stroke more sympathetic with the background.

Once you've finished, **Save** the **Smart Object** (or just close the window, and you'll be prompted to save it). The artwork will now be updated in the texture layer, and you'll see it appear on your 3D postcard.

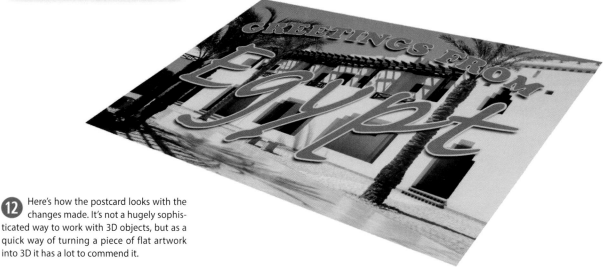

12 Here's how the postcard looks with the changes made. It's not a hugely sophisticated way to work with 3D objects, but as a quick way of turning a piece of flat artwork into 3D it has a lot to commend it.

6 3D presets

3D PRESETS are basic 3D shapes that come ready-made for immediate use. No need to draw an outline or begin with a photograph; primitives can be created on the fly and pressed into service straight away.

Having said that, some primitives have more sophistication and more wide-reaching possibilities, such as the bottle composed of three parts or the texture-wrappable cube. As with so much in Photoshop, there's more to primitives than at first meets the eye.

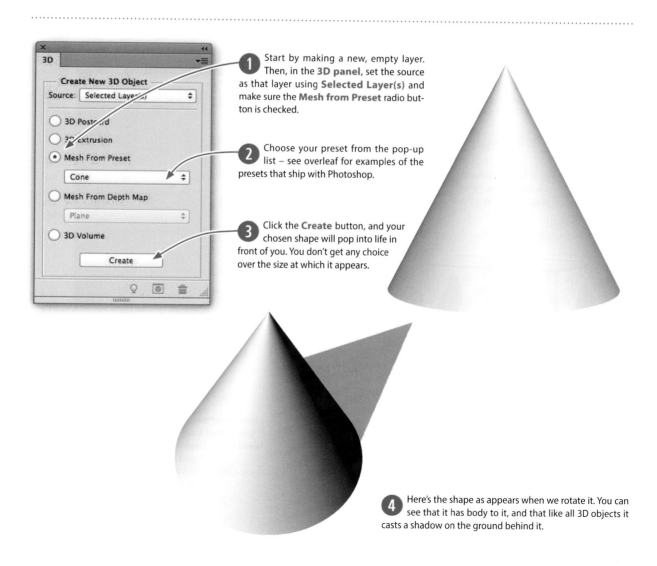

1 Start by making a new, empty layer. Then, in the **3D panel**, set the source as that layer using **Selected Layer(s)** and make sure the **Mesh from Preset** radio button is checked.

2 Choose your preset from the pop-up list – see overleaf for examples of the presets that ship with Photoshop.

3 Click the **Create** button, and your chosen shape will pop into life in front of you. You don't get any choice over the size at which it appears.

4 Here's the shape as appears when we rotate it. You can see that it has body to it, and that like all 3D objects it casts a shadow on the ground behind it.

Basic primitives

THERE ARE TWO KINDS of preset shapes: the first batch comprises the so-called *primitives*, based on the geometric forms laid down by Plato a couple of thousand years ago. As with all preset objects, you can move, rotate and scale them, but you can't apply any of the other distortions to them – so you can't take a cone and taper it into a spiral, for instance.

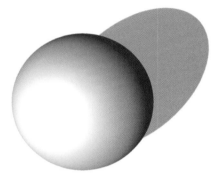

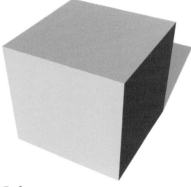

Sphere
The most basic shape of all. It's perfect for creating pool balls, soccer balls and tennis balls, of course, but is also ideal for wrapping maps around to make rotatable globes.

Cube
Although it defaults to a true cube that's of equal length on all sides, it can be stretched to make any shape of cuboid. It's a good basis for making boxes of any dimension.

Donut
More properly known as a **torus**, this ring shape is less useful than it might be due to our inability to change its inner radius. You're better off creating a torus manually.

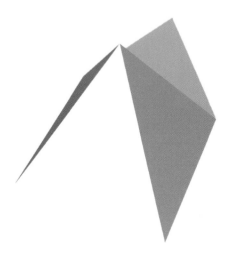

Cylinder
Unlike the torus, we're able to scale both the height and the radius of this cylinder, which means it can be used for a variety of purposes: as a signpost, a gun barrel, a table leg, and much more – especially when combined with other objects as part of a complex scene.

Pyramid
When you first make a pyramid, it looks like the operation hasn't happened. That's because the default view is of just the front face, which appears so brightly lit that it's pure white.

But don't give up – the pyramid really is there. All you have to do is to rotate the view to show it from a different angle.

Complex presets

AS WELL AS PLATONIC PRIMITIVES, Photoshop includes a small and slightly odd range of additional models. The wine bottle is a good shape, and the soda can can be useful; but the ring is a strange choice. Not as strange, though, as that bizarre hat, which seems to serve no real purpose. I suppose you could stick it on someone's head if you were really desperate.

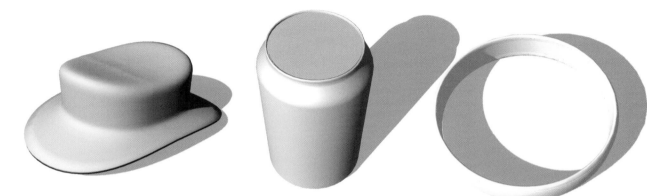

Hat
But not really a hat as we'd know it. Of all the objects in the world to choose, I can't imagine what prompted Adobe to pick this one. Do let me know if you find a use for it.

Soda can
It may not look like much on its own, but when you wrap a label around the soda can (as we'll see later in this book), it can become a container for just about any kind of drink.

Ring
A curious object, the ring is the only 3D preset shape to come with a material attached – in this case, it's a shiny gold. It's hard to find a good use for it, though.

Cube Wrap and Spherical Panorama
These two shapes are designed to work in very specific ways when textures are added, and don't look like anything much on their own. We'll be looking at how to work with them in more detail later in this chapter.

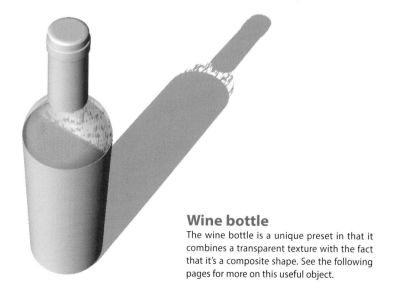

Wine bottle
The wine bottle is a unique preset in that it combines a transparent texture with the fact that it's a composite shape. See the following pages for more on this useful object.

Not-so-primitive bottle

AS I SAID ON THE PREVIOUS PAGE, the Wine Bottle is unique among Photoshop's 3D presets in that it's not just a simple basic shape but a complete, finished object composed of a number of separate elements. And unlike the Ring or the Donut, we're able to dig in and edit each part.

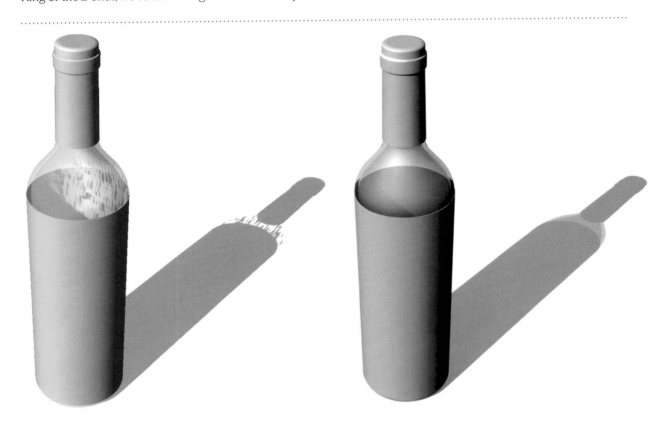

1 When you choose Wine Bottle from the pop-up list of 3D presets, you first see it head-on: here, I've rotated it to a different angle so we're looking down on it more.

Right away, you can see it isn't a regular preset. For one thing, there's a dappled quality to the glass area, which gives the first clue that there's something rather special about it.

2 When the bottle is **rendered**, we can see that the transparent area takes on a glossy, truly glass-like appearance. (We haven't covered rendering 3D scenes yet – see Chapter 9).

Note how not only the glass but its shadow is translucent, allowing the light to shine through. Note, also, how the rendered view shows the back side of the label distorting with refraction as it's viewed through the glass: this is clear in the rendered version, but not in the standard preview.

It's very easy to make objects partially transparent in Photoshop, and to set the amount of their refraction, and we'll be looking at both of these factors in detail in Chapter 13.

3 Look at the **3D panel** and you'll see that the bottle is in fact made of three different objects.

You can select each of the objects independently, and move them around, just as I've moved the label out to the side here.

4 Because each element is a separate object, we're able to change the appearance of each one. We can recolor the cap, to make it a more appropriate red; we can change the color of the glass itself; and we can design a new label and place it on the bottle.

Another important factor is the ability to change an object's scale. So here I've adjusted just the height of the label, using the **Head-Up Controls**, to make it more appropriate for the bottle.

Wrapping textures around cubes

WE HAVEN'T LOOKED at textures yet, but when creating objects from presets, if a layer already has a texture on it, then that texture will be applied to the object when it's created.

Just how that texture is made isn't always intuitive, and varies from object to object. Here, we'll look at how textures work when applied to both the Cube and the Cube Wrap presets.

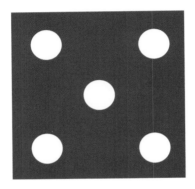

1 We'll use this simple dice texture as the basis for a new 3D layer. From the **3D panel**, check the **Mesh from Preset** button and choose **Cube** as the object type.

Then, as usual, all you have to do is to hit the **Create** button

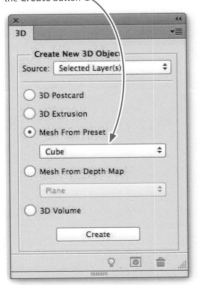

2 Here's the result: the layer is turned into a cube, and the artwork that constituted the layer is mapped onto the front face of that cube. As with some other preset object creation, you'll need to rotate the object before you can see that it really is three-dimensional.

You'll notice that only the front face of the cube holds the texture; the remaining faces are blank. If you want to map artwork onto them, you'll have to choose the **Cube Wrap** preset instead – so let's do that next.

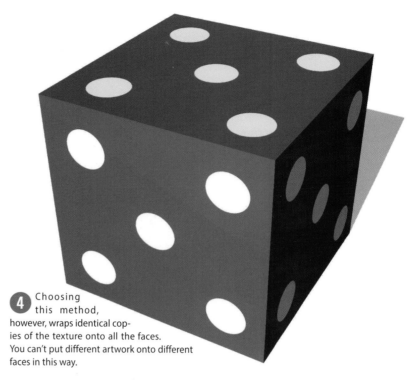

3 Proceed as before, except this time select **Cube Wrap** as the preset type before going on to click the **Create** button.

This time, the texture is wrapped around all the faces of the cube, matching them all precisely and filling them in an exactly equal way.

4 Choosing this method, however, wraps identical copies of the texture onto all the faces. You can't put different artwork onto different faces in this way.

5 Whenever you create a 3D layer from a preset, the entire canvas area of the image is used. Here, the canvas has been enlarged so that the dice artwork is in the middle, surrounded by a landscape-shaped empty image.

6 Selecting **Cube Wrap** reshapes the artwork to fit the cube, not the other way around. So the whole canvas has been reshaped to square, and the empty area around the dice design has been replaced with a mid-tone gray.

Adding textures around other presets

WE'LL LOOK AT TEXTURES MORE in the next section of the book, but for now let's finish this chapter with a quick look at what happens when you create preset 3D layers from layers that already contain artwork. Each object behaves slightly differently, and it's useful to know what's going to happen so you know how to prepare the artwork beforehand.

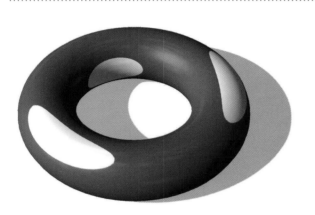

1 Most of the preset objects will simply take the texture and wrap it around the entire object, distorting it as necessary to fit the shape. So the **Donut**, above, and the **Cone**, right, have squeezed the dice image to fit the surface to which it has been applied.

2 The more sophisticated presets behave in a different way. When making a 3D layer that uses existing artwork as its basis, both the **Wine Bottle** (left) and the **Soda Can** (right) have been designed so that the artwork is applied only to the label area.

When working with the wine bottle, as we've seen, we're able to modify the size of the label as it's essentially a separate object within the wame 3D layer. But the soda can doesn't give us that same ability; all we can do is wrap the artwork around the whole can (although the top and base are left blank).

7 Other creation tools

DEPTH MAPS are a method of creating 3D objects from flat artwork, in which white appears high and black appears low. Although they might seem more primitive than the methods we've so far been using for creating our artwork, they offer a lot of flexibility with the potential for expressive design.

There are a couple of other, more specialized tools for building 3D objects – Spherical Panoramas, 3D Volumes and a way of making 3D objects using the Vanishing Point filter. We'll look at all of these as well.

1 Start by creating a simple rectangular shape, on a new layer, filled with a mid-gray. Add two words on top of this – *High*, set in white, and *Low*, set in black.

You can use any font you like, but a simple, uncluttered sans serif will work best. I've used Arial Rounded because its soft corners are particularly well suited to extrusion in this manner.

2 You'll see that the white text, black text and gray background form three separate layers. Select all three in the **Layers panel** by clicking on the top one and then holding **Shift** as you click on the bottom one. Choose **Layer > Merge Layers** to turn them all into a single layer.

3 In the **3D panel**, set the **Source** as **Selected Layer**, and check the **Mesh from Depth Map** radio button. Choose **Plane** from the pop-up menu beneath it, and then click the **Create** button ●

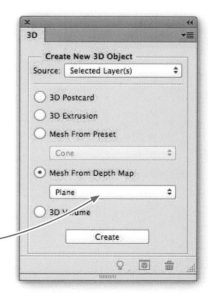

The Depth Map mesh

4 When you click **Create** you'll see that the layer has been turned into a three-dimensional object. The plain gray layer forms the base, out of which the word *High* is extruded toward us, and the word *Low* is recessed away from us.

Depth maps produce 3D objects entirely based on the brightness value of the pixels in the artwork they're generated from. We've worked in shades of gray, rather than in colors, so the effect can be seen more clearly.

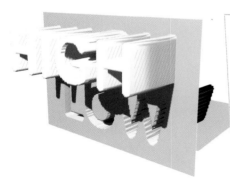

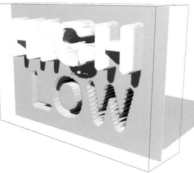

5 When the object is spun around, you can see the effect more clearly. The word *High* projects forward a long way, and you can see how recessed the word *Low* is: it's so deep you can just make out the end of the *w* projecting out of the back of the object.

6 Unlike regular extruded objects, there are no **Head-Up Display** controls to control the depth. Instead, we have to use the **3D Axis** controller to manipulate it.

By dragging the **Scale Along Z** control (the small blue cube at the end of the Z-axis arm), we can make the whole object thinner.

7 As well as selecting the regular **Plane** mesh, you can choose the **Two-Sided Plane**. This replicates the artwork in reverse on both sides, reproducing it to make a double-sided mesh.

Note that the mesh isn't reproduced in the same way on the back of the mesh; it's more as if it has been reflected in a three-dimensional mirror.

Smoothing the mesh

THE TROUBLE WITH DEPTH MAPS is that the meshes they produce can appear very harsh: you'll notice how ragged the words *High* and *Low* look in the example we've been using. That's partly due to the sheer height of the extrusion, but we can help it out with a little judicious smoothing.

1 In the **Properties panel**, make sure the **Mesh** pane is selected (the other button is for the Coordinates) and then click the **Edit Source** button.

This will open the original artwork in a new window. If you have Photoshop set up to open windows in tabs, then drag it out to the side so you can see both windows at the same time.

2 Press the **/** key to lock the transparency of the layer, then choose **Filter > Blur > Gaussian Blur**. I've used a blur amount of 8 pixels here.

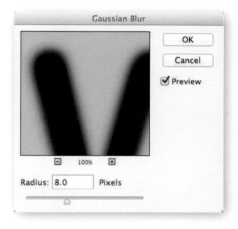

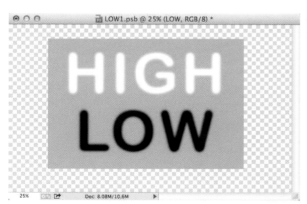

3 You'll see a result something like this. Note that I've reduced the size of the artwork window so the 3D object is clearly visible in the window behind it.

After trying a blur, **Save** the new .psb window (**File > Save**) and the changes will take immediate effect in the 3D object behind.

4 Here's the result: the blur process has softened the text, smoothing off the harsh edges. It has also made the sides of the letters slope at more of an angle, which is why *High* appears thinner and *Low* thicker.

Cylinders from depth maps

DEPTH MAPS CAN PRODUCE a small selection of shapes, including – as we see here – a cylinder. We'll use the same artwork we used for the plane to show how to change the depth of the effect on the cylinder: it's a rather different process than working with the plane.

1 Set the **Source** to **Selected Layer**, and make sure the **Mesh from Depth Map** radio button is checked; then choose **Cylinder** from the pop-up list, and click the **Create** button.

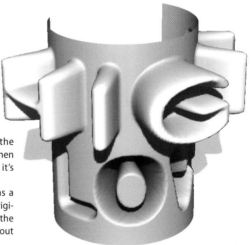

2 Here's the result. It's much the same as the effect produced when we created the plane, except that it's wrapped around a cylinder.

You'll notice that the cylinder has a gap at the back. That's because the original artwork wasn't the full width of the canvas; to get rid of the gap, stretch out the artwork first.

3 As before, the problem is that the extruded letters are far too deep. Previously, we were able to make the plane less thick by dragging on the Z-axis scale in the **3D Axis** controller.

But we can't do that this time: when we try to scale along just one axis, it's not just the lettering that gets squeezed but the whole cylinder, resulting in this ugly distortion.

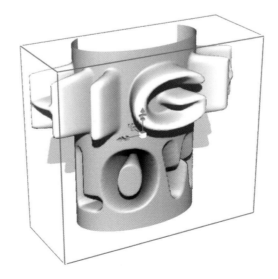

4 The solution is to reduce the contrast on the original artwork. As before, click the **Edit Source** button on the **Properties panel** to open the base artwork in a new **.psb** window.

5 Use **Image** > **Adjustments** > **Curves** to open the Curves dialog, then drag the bottom left point vertically. This makes the dark areas brighter

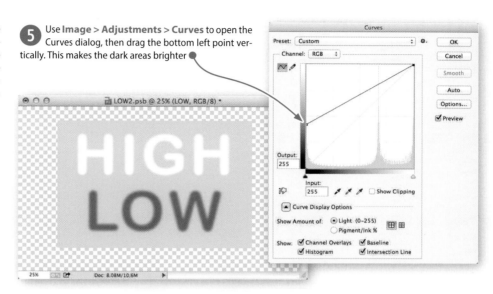

6 Now drag the top right point of the curve vertically downward. This makes the bright areas darker

Click OK to apply the adjustment, then **Save** the .psb document and the changes will immediately be reflected in the 3D object.

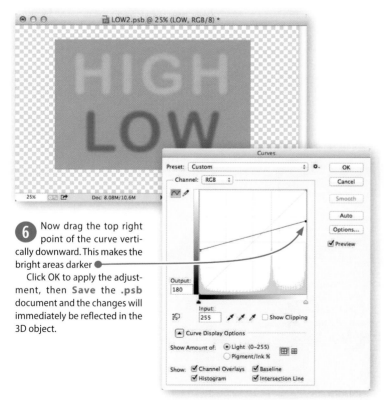

7 Here's the result: the text is a lot less prominent. You can adjust the balance as much as you like by tinkering with the contrast of the artwork.

Texture and color

ALL THE DEPTH MAPS we've created so far have been grayscale images, with no color component. But Photoshop can also work with color images, and it uses them in two ways: first as a depth map, to provide the height of the surface, and second, as a texture to tint that surface.

Although the texture serves a dual purpose here, we're able to modify one use of it (as a depth map) without affecting the other (as a surface texture).

1 This simple drawing features a wavy blue "sky" over a greenish "ground." Inset at the bottom are three purple circles arranged in a line.

From a depth map point of view, the color is irrelevant: all it's going to look at is the variation in *luminosity*, or the brightness value of each pixel it encounters.

As before, set **Cylinder** as the mesh type, and click the **Create** button.

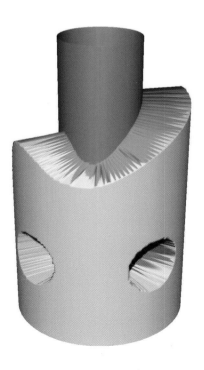

2 Here's the result of that operation. The dark blue is low, and the bright green is high: and those purple dots are so recessed we can barely see the color.

The edges are very hard, though, and there are strong striations of color on the extruded surfaces. That's because the hard divide between the colors means the color changes are stretched over a tiny distance.

We can fix that by blurring the depth map. This will soften the transition between the high and low areas, giving the color more of a surface area to sit on.

3 Open the **Layers panel**, and you'll see how the texture has been used throughout this image.

Ignore the **Diffuse** texture, which is the color component, and the **Image Based Light** (we'll look at this later in this book), and instead double-click the **Layer 1 Depth Map** ●

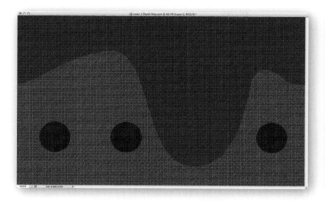

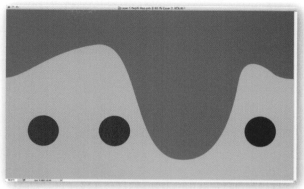

4 When you double-click the **Layer 1 Depth Map** in the **Layers panel**, it will open in a new **.psb** window. You'll see this grid overlaid on it: you can hide the grid using **View > Show > UV Overlay**.

5 Here's the image without that UV Overlay. Although it can be useful when you want to see how the underlying surface is constructed, in most cases it just gets in the way.

6 Use **Filter > Blur > Gaussian Blur** to soften the image. I've used a Radius of 20 pixels here, but the value you choose depends on the size of the artwork you started with.

Try a number at random, or just drag the slider, and then click **OK**. When you **Save** the .psb file you'll see the change it's made to the 3D object; if it doesn't look right, then **Undo** and use ⌘ ⌥ F ctrl alt F to open the filter dialog again, so you can try a different value.

Remember to **Save** the .psb to apply the texture to the model.

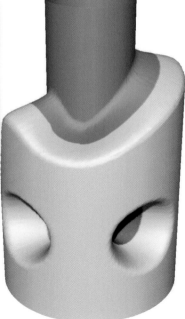

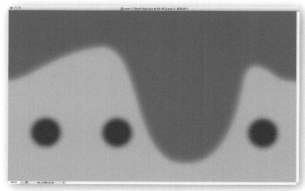

7 Here's the result of smoothing the depth map. Note how the sides of the purple dot holes are sloping: the width of the slope is 20 pixels, the amount of the Gaussian Blur.

Note, too, how the color itself has not blurred. That's because we only blurred the depth map, not the diffuse texture. The transition between blue and green is exactly halfway along the slope in the model.

Build your own planet

YOU CAN'T CREATE many kinds of meshes from depth maps, but one of the most interesting ones is the Sphere. Apart from using it to make pool balls and sports objects of all kinds, we can use it to construct planets. Here's a straightforward way to make a rotatable Earth.

1 Here's a simple map of the world, using the standard Mercator projection. It's important to use this projection rather than, say, Robinson, as it will produce the best results when wrapped around a sphere.

I found this map in black and white, as an Adobe Illustrator object, and opened it in Photoshop. We'll need to color it in.

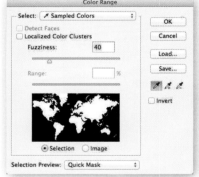

2 We want to color in this map, but we want to color the land and the sea separately.

Begin by choosing **Select > Color Range**, and this dialog will appear. Click on the land, and you should see the land area selected in white in the preview inside the dialog.

Depending on what you have chosen in the **Selection Preview** pop-up menu at the bottom of the dialog, you'll see the selection on the image in a variety of ways; here it is shown as a **QuickMask** preview.

3 Click **OK** to make the selection, then open the **Swatches panel**. Select a pale green, and use ⌘ ⌥ Backspace ctrl alt Backspace to fill the selected area with that color.

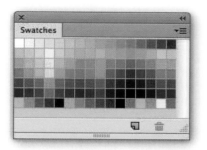

4 Now for the sea. Use **Select > Inverse** (or press ⌘ Shift I ctrl Shift I) so that the sea, and not the land, is selected. Choose a blue color, and use ⌘ ⌥ Backspace ctrl alt Backspace in the same way to fill the selection with that color.

Keyboard shortcuts MAC WIN BOTH

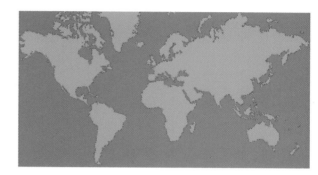

5 In the **3D panel**, choose **Sphere** in the **Mesh from Depth Map** pop-up menu, then click the **Create** button.

You'll see something like this. The map will have wrapped itself around a sphere, but it's likely that the difference between land and sea will be greatly exaggerated.

We'll see how to fix that next.

Adjusting the contrast

6 Open the **Layers panel** and double-click the **Depth Map** at the bottom, and the image will appear in a new **.psb** window. As we saw in the cylinder example, it may open with a grid overlay; turn this off using **View > Show > UV Overlay**. You'll now see the original map, exactly as we colored it.

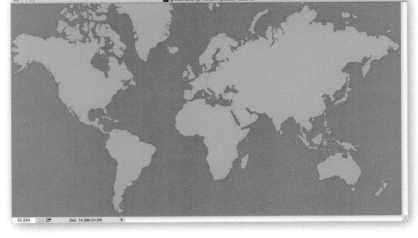

7 Use **Select > Color Range** once more to make the selection – but this time, select the sea area rather than the land. Even though we've now colored the land and sea, it's still possible to make an accurate selection using the difference in color between the two.

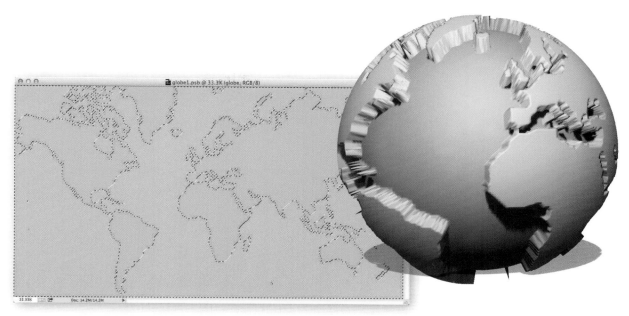

8 Use the **Curves** or the **Levels** dialog, whichever you prefer, to brighten that sea area, then press ⌘ S *ctrl* S to **Save** the **.psb** document. This will instantly update the globe we've built.

As you can see, the effect is still much too extreme: the land is still too high. Use the adjustment again to make the sea even brighter, then **Save** again; keep repeating this process until you get a more plausible land-sea height difference.

9 Here's the image with the contrast correctly adjusted: this produces the subtle globe effect we were after. As you can see, the land and sea are almost exactly the same color. It doesn't take much variation in luminosity to create the height map.

It's worth noting that although the sea is much brighter in the depth map, the color of the sea on the planet remains the same deep blue. That's because we haven't changed the diffuse texture, just the depth map.

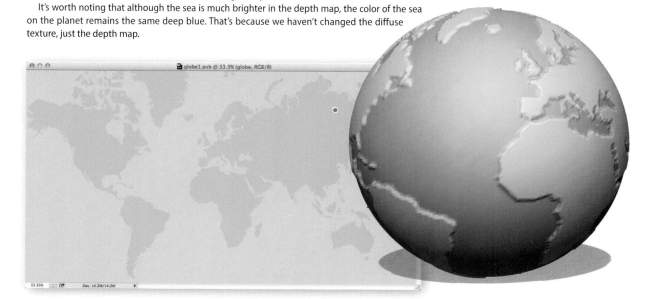

Spherical panoramas

A SPHERICAL PANORAMA is a tool for mapping panoramic images around a sphere to create a virtual environment that the user can pan around and examine in detail. Creating the panoramic images is beyond the scope of this book – but see www.panoramaphotographer.com for more expert images from Keith Martin, who photographed and assembled the scene below.

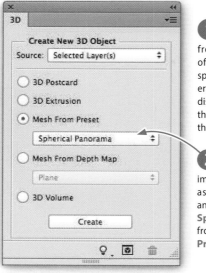

1 The scene above has been created from multiple shots of the scene, using a specially adapted camera. Note the apparent distortion, especially of that black chair right in the middle of the scene.

2 After opening your panoramic image, set the **Source** as **Selected Layer** and choose the preset **Spherical Panorama** from the **Mesh from Preset** pop-up menu.

3 Here's the result: we're presented with a close-up view of part of the wall in the image. We can navigate around this view using the standard 3D **Move tool**.

4 When we zoom out of the image we can see more of the room, as the spherical panorama comes into play.

5 As we pan around the image, we can see that most of the apparent distortion is hidden when we look up and down.

6 Looking down at that highly distorted chair, for example, now reveals it and the desk behind in undistorted form.

7 If we continue to zoom out, we suddenly find ourselves moving through the opposite wall to the one we were looking at.

8 Here's what's happening: the panorama is actually wrapped around a sphere, which we were examining from the *inside*. That's how the panoramic effect is produced: wherever we turn we're surrounded by the interior of the sphere, producing the illusion of a wholly submersive, surrounding environment.

3D from Vanishing Point

THE VANISHING POINT filter allows Photoshop users to define perspective planes within an image, and then to clone onto or paste artwork onto those planes. The cloned or copied artwork will be applied in the same perspective as the original photograph. But there's another side to the filter – its ability to generate workable 3D models.

1 This stack of books is cut away from its background, and comes courtesy of the photo library **absolutvision.com**. You can download this image at **3DPhotoshop.net**.

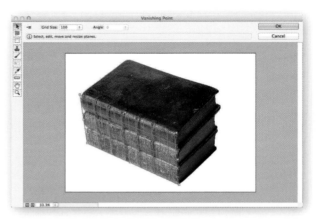

2 Open the image in Photoshop, and choose **Vanishing Point** from the top of the **Filter** menu. It will open a new window. Click to mark four corners of a plane that matches the back of the books: you'll see a blue grid appear when you've marked the points correctly.

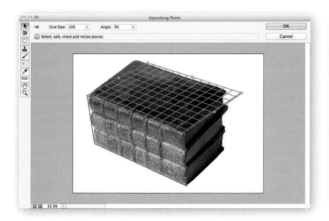

3 When you've got one side complete, hold ⌘ ctrl and drag on the middle handle on the top edge to "tear off" another plane at right angles to the first.

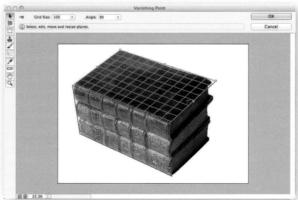

4 The new plane almost certainly won't match the shape – but you can correct it by dragging the two free corners (that is, those that aren't attached to the first plane). If the grid turns red or yellow, it's an "illegal" plane; adjust it until it turns blue again.

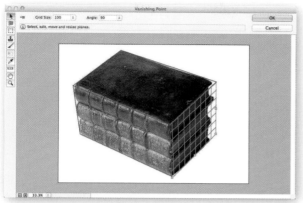

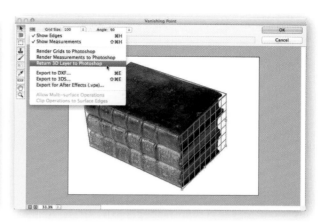

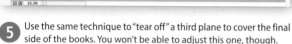

5 Use the same technique to "tear off" a third plane to cover the final side of the books. You won't be able to adjust this one, though.

6 From the tiny icon at top left, choose **Return 3D Layer to Photoshop**. Then click **OK**.

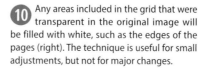

7 When you exit the dialog, you'll see that the books look very much as they did before you started the operation.

8 But in fact those books are now a 3D object, which can be turned around and viewed from different directions, using the **Move tool**. And if you look in the **Layers panel**, you'll see the books appearing as a standard 3D layer.

9 There are severe limitations to the technique. For one thing, the books are hollow: only three faces will have been modeled, as you'll see if you turn it around (left).

10 Any areas included in the grid that were transparent in the original image will be filled with white, such as the edges of the pages (right). The technique is useful for small adjustments, but not for major changes.

The problem with 3D volume

SITTING RIGHT AT THE BOTTOM of the 3D panel is the 3D Volume button, and of course it's tempting to click it to see what happens. But the 3D Volume control is designed for converting medical DICOM images into viewable objects, and unless you happen to be a brain surgeon, you're likely to find it less than enthralling.

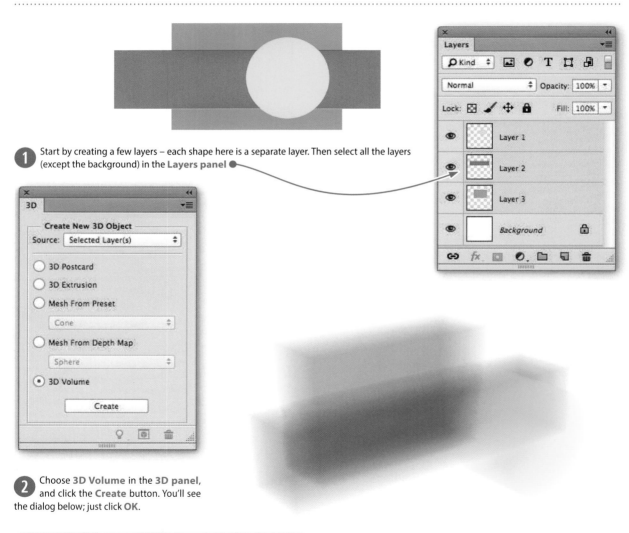

1 Start by creating a few layers – each shape here is a separate layer. Then select all the layers (except the background) in the **Layers panel** ●

2 Choose **3D Volume** in the **3D panel**, and click the **Create** button. You'll see the dialog below; just click **OK**.

3 And here's the result: a rather fuzzy extrusion of the three layers. You can rotate it, but you can't scale it or drag it around the workspace, or reshape it in any way.

I've tried experimenting with all kinds of images created in Photoshop, and I've yet to find a creative use for this technique.

8 Importing 3D objects

THE EASIEST WAY to make a 3D model in Photoshop should be to import one from elsewhere. Photoshop is able to handle a variety of 3D formats, featuring most popular file types – and even including types such as .kmz, used by Google Sketchup, and the 3D printing format .stl.

But importing 3D models isn't always straightforward. In this chapter we'll look at how to import and manipulate 3D objects, and we'll take a look at what happens when importing goes wrong.

Photoshop can import a range of 3D model formats, but by no means all the formats that are available. The list on the right shows the file types Photoshop can currently work with.

If you want to use files in a different format from those listed, there are applications that will convert between the various formats for you.

OBJ	Wavefront .obj format, the most common interchange format for models.
3D Studio	.3ds, the native format for models created with Autodesk 3ds Max.
Collada DAE	A 3D interchange adopted by ISO as a public model specification.
Flash 3D	The format used by Adobe Flash for interactive 3D models on websites.
KMZ	The native format used by Google Earth, for models made in Sketchup.
STL	The stereolithography CAD format from by 3D Systems, used for 3D printing.

This model of the Galileo space probe would be almost impossible to model directly in Photoshop – it's far too complex and too fiddly. But it's one of the many public domain models offered as a download from the NASA website, allowing us to create detailed scenes with ease. The background is also from the NASA image library, completing the picture.

NASA comes to town

IF YOU WANT SPACE MODELS, then the NASA website should be your first port of call. There's a range of about 140 models, from the Gemini spacecraft up to the Hubble space telescope – as well as a set of models of astronauts and their equipment.

All the models are free for you to download and use in your own projects. If you live in the United States, then this is because you've already paid for them out of your taxes. And if that is the case, then thanks. The rest of us are just freeloading.

1 Visit **www.nasa.gov/multimedia/3d_resources/models.html** to see the range of models NASA makes available. Scroll through the list, and click on the model you want to work with.

Before you download it, however, check its file format. A lot of the later models are in the native **Blender** format, which means they have not been exported from that program in a usable state. You can always download Blender yourself from **blender.org** – it's a free, open source program – import the downloaded model, and then export it yourself in a format Photoshop can use. But if you want to avoid this extra step, stick to models in **.3DS** or **.OBJ** formats.

We're going to work with a handheld, pistol-like tool downloaded from the NASA website. You can download it from **1.usa.gov/XT8QuN**.

2 To get started, either **Open** the downloaded file, or make a new document and choose **New 3D Layer from File** from Photoshop's **3D** menu.

3 When we turn the object around by selecting it and spinning it with the **Move tool**, we can see that it's a real 3D object. It comes ready-made with a set of textures, and you can see how they have been mapped onto the body of the tool.

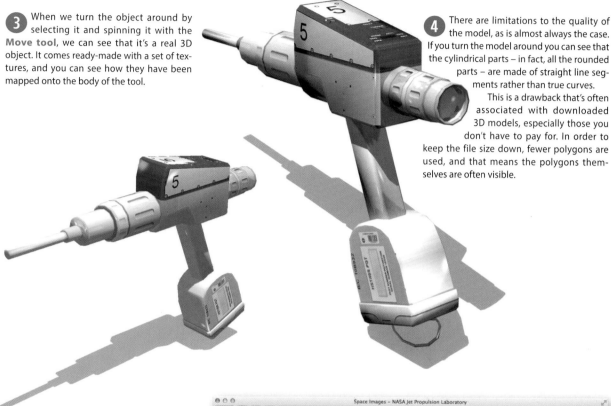

4 There are limitations to the quality of the model, as is almost always the case. If you turn the model around you can see that the cylindrical parts – in fact, all the rounded parts – are made of straight line segments rather than true curves.

This is a drawback that's often associated with downloaded 3D models, especially those you don't have to pay for. In order to keep the file size down, fewer polygons are used, and that means the polygons themselves are often visible.

5 If you want space backgrounds for your images, check out NASA's collection of free-to-use shots of space, planets and everything in between at **www.jpl.nasa.gov**.

For a wider range of image types (but somewhat trickier image search), then there are links from the main NASA site to a range of libraries at **www.nasa.gov/multimedia/imagegallery/index.html**.

Google 3D Warehouse

GOOGLE 3D WAREHOUSE was designed as a repository for 3D buildings created for Google Earth, using the 3D modeler Google Sketchup. Sketchup has now been sold to the developer Trimble, with the result that although the URL is still sketchup.google.com/3dwarehouse, the site is now officially called *Trimble 3D Warehouse powered by Google*. Nonetheless, the site still includes a good selection of 3D models, the best being architectural; you can also find a huge range of other models too, but of variable quality.

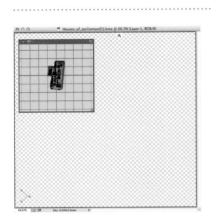

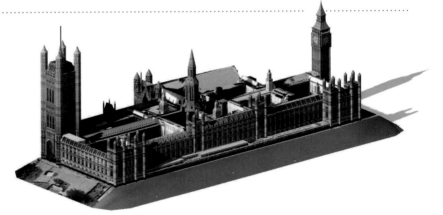

1 This model of London's Houses of Parliament can be downloaded here:

bit.ly/14Spzm2

When you open the model, it appears to be entirely missing. But check the **Secondary View**: it is there, but off camera somewhere.

2 Click the button to swap the main and secondary views to see it in the Photoshop window

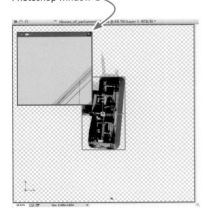

3 The model is made of a great many parts, as you'd expect from a building of this complexity. To move it around, select the *Model* group in the **3D panel** rather than just clicking on it with the **Move tool**, or you'll find you'll only be moving a section of the building.

4 Although the model is very complete, it does appear rather flat and unrealistic. That's all because of the way the **camera** is set up.

To fix this, click the **Current View** item in the **3D panel**, to open its settings.

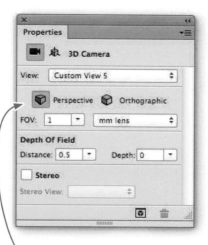

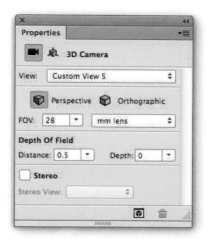

5 The reason the model looks a little stilted is because the view is set to **Orthographic**, rather than **Perspective**.

This view shows all verticals as true verticals, without any of the simulated lens distortion that makes 3D models look more like their real-world counterparts.

6 Click the button marked **Perspective** to change the view to one we're more used to.

You'll see something rather bizarre happening: the model suddenly shrinks to a tiny size. That's because in switching views, Photoshop has set the *Field of View* (**FOV**) to 1, and this results in a camera that would be impossible to build as a real item.

7 Changing the **Field of View** will make the model look more realistic once more. Here, I've set the value to simulate a 28mm lens, resulting in the view of the building seen below.

8 This model is composed of a great many parts – and an equal number of textures, many of them faithfully photographed from the building itself. The view of the **Layers panel** on the left is too small to read, but shows the number of textures involved.

The more complex a model is, the more chance there is for things to go wrong. When rendering this model, the textures on the top of the clock tower become slightly misaligned: it is possible to fix, if you can track down the texture that needs to be amended.

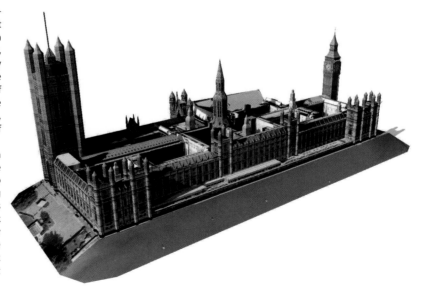

Daz Studio

DAZ STUDIO 4 is a 3D modeling environment that acts as a front end for the vast Daz3D collection of human, robotic and animal figures – and it's a free download from **www.daz3d.com**. What makes Daz Studio different is its ability not just to import 3D models, but to *pose* them: all the figures can be positioned in just about any pose you can imagine. It's a terrific way to bring both people and animals into your Photoshop scenes.

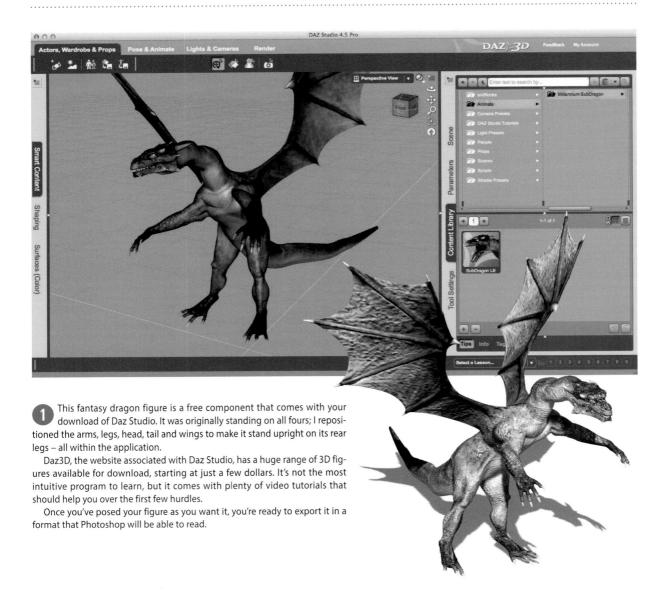

1 This fantasy dragon figure is a free component that comes with your download of Daz Studio. It was originally standing on all fours; I repositioned the arms, legs, head, tail and wings to make it stand upright on its rear legs – all within the application.

Daz3D, the website associated with Daz Studio, has a huge range of 3D figures available for download, starting at just a few dollars. It's not the most intuitive program to learn, but it comes with plenty of video tutorials that should help you over the first few hurdles.

Once you've posed your figure as you want it, you're ready to export it in a format that Photoshop will be able to read.

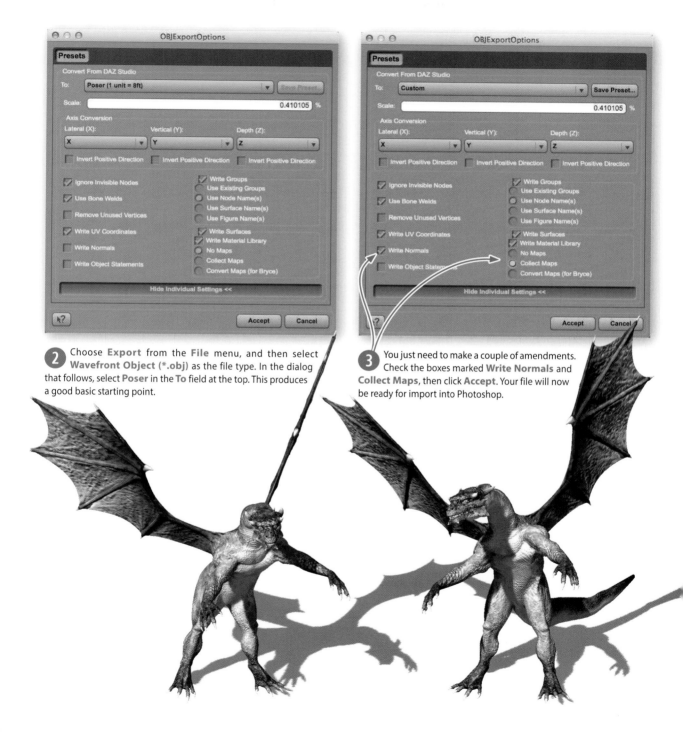

2 Choose **Export** from the **File** menu, and then select **Wavefront Object (*.obj)** as the file type. In the dialog that follows, select **Poser** in the **To** field at the top. This produces a good basic starting point.

3 You just need to make a couple of amendments. Check the boxes marked **Write Normals** and **Collect Maps**, then click **Accept**. Your file will now be ready for import into Photoshop.

Daz Studio issues

DAZ STUDIO 4 is a terrific (and free) tool, but there are some potential problems when exporting models to be used in a Photoshop document. Here, we'll look at how to solve some of those problems – as well as one that's much harder to solve.

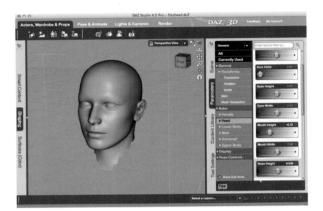

1 This head was modeled in Daz Studio by hiding all the other body parts. It was then exported as an **OBJ** file.

When imported into Photoshop, it appears much too bleached out. The first step is to reduce the brightness of the whole model.

You can download this head model from **3DPhotoshop.net**.

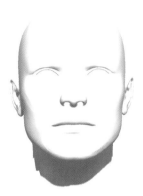

2 To lower the overall brightness, click twice on the model to open the **Materials** pane of the **Properties panel**, then click the color swatch next to the word **Specular**. This will open the **Color Picker**, so we can lower its brightness.

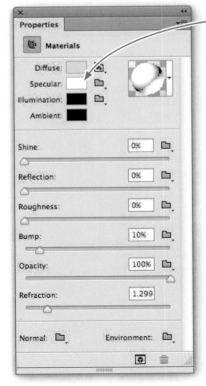

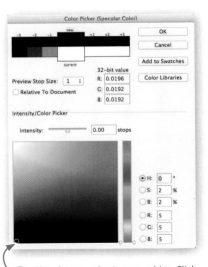

3 The chosen color is pure white. Click down in the bottom-left corner of the picker to change the color to black, to hide the Specular effect.

4 Here's the result: that over-bright model is now much more reasonably lit, and we can see the shading on the face much more clearly.

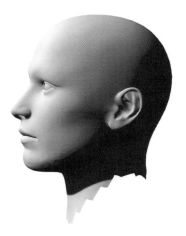

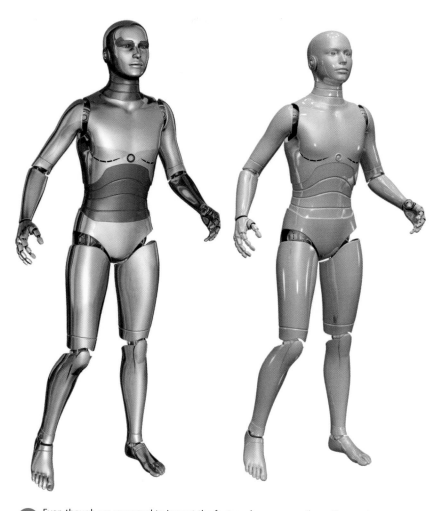

5 When we turn the model around, we can see the jagged edge of the neck. That's because Daz Studio expects it to have a body attached.

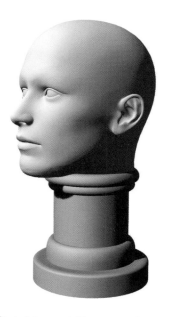

6 As it turns out, it's easy to make a new object as a plinth and attach it to the head. We'll look at how to combine 3D layers in part three of this book.

7 Even though we managed to import the fantasy dragon correctly on the previous pages, with all its textures intact, some features don't make it across during the transition from Daz Studio to Photoshop.

This robotic figure was created for Daz Studio, and on the left is the final render made in that program. As well as being lightning fast, it has produced a strong sense of shine and reflection, resulting in a very fine finished image.

The figure on the left is the result of exporting the model from Daz Studio and importing it into Photoshop. Despite having increased both the Reflection and the Shine amounts, it still looks dull and plastic in comparison with the original.

It would probably be possible to adjust all the texture and surface properties to make the figure match the original, but it would be a lot of work – and then when the figure's pose is changed, we'd have to go through the process all over again. Sometimes, it makes sense just to render in Daz Studio, and then composite the still image in Photoshop.

The multiple object problem

THIS MODEL COMES from www.3dm3.com, a good repository of free downloadable 3D models. The vagaries of 3D model creation means that sometimes they aren't formatted precisely as we'd like in order to be able to work with them directly in Photoshop.

Sometimes the problem is impossible to fix, as we'll see later in this chapter; sometimes all it takes is a straightforward and easy correction.

1 When we first open this fan in Photoshop, it looks absolutely fine: it's a head-on view and nothing seems out of place. You can download the fan here:

bit.ly/ZEY00J

The difficulty becomes apparent when we try to work with this model. All is not exactly as it seems.

2 The first step in working with any 3D object, of course, is to select it. But when we click on this object we can see that only the bottom part of it is selected – the bounding box, tinted pale yellow to show the selection area more clearly, doesn't extend as far as the fan blades or their surround.

If we tried to manipulate the model as it stands, we'd end up just moving the base around, and we'd leave the rest of the fan out in limbo.

3 A glance at the **3D panel** shows what's going on. The fan has been built in three separate parts, named *Feather*, *Fan* and *Curve*; each one has its own coloring and textures attached.

One way to solve this would be simply to select each of the three elements, by clicking on the top one (*Feather*) and holding *Shift* as we click on the bottom one (*Curve*).

But we'd have to remember to do that each time we wanted to move the fan; it would be awkward to have to do so on each occasion, or risk it all falling apart.

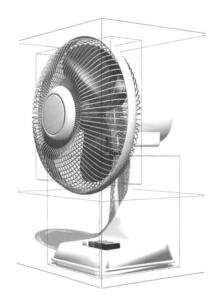

4 Fortunately – and naturally, as you'd expect in Photoshop – there's a solution. Select all three layers as described in the previous step, then click on the pop-up menu at the top right of the **3D panel**.

Choose **Group Objects** from this menu, and all three will be placed within a single folder, just as if you were creating a regular Layer Group in Photoshop.

All you have to do now is remember to select the group when you want to manipulate the fan. If you like, you can click the arrow to the left of the Group icon to close it, and it will appear as just a single object.

When you click on any one object in the group you'll still be able to select it individually, but at least it's now easier to modify the entire group as a whole.

5 The fan may look like an artificial construction when viewed on its own, but when it's dropped into a room setting – as it is below – it blends in perfectly. Later in this book we'll look at adjusting lighting and rendering models, which enables us to produce realistic images.

The benefit of multiple objects

WE'VE ALREADY LOOKED at how imported 3D models often appear in multiple parts, and the problems that can cause. But there's an upside to this as well, in that it allows us to manipulate elements of a model independently of each other.

The model we're going to work with here comes from archive3d.net, a vast and splendid collection of free-to-use 3D models.

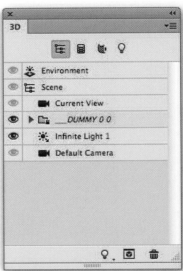

1 This music stand opens head-on in Photoshop – I've added a background so it's clearer to see. You can download the music stand here:

bit.ly/14S57S1

Let's see what happens when we try to manipulate this object.

2 Using the **Move tool** to manipulate the object works just as we'd expect: the whole music stand moves as one, even though it's composed of multiple parts.

3 We can see why when we look at the **3D panel**. The designer of this object has already placed all the elements into a single folder – even if he has given it the rather odd name __DUMMY 0 0.

So when we click on the object with the **Move tool**, we're automatically selecting the whole folder rather than just a part of it.

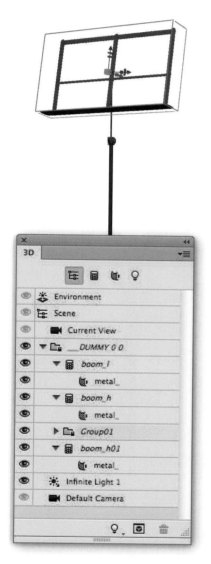

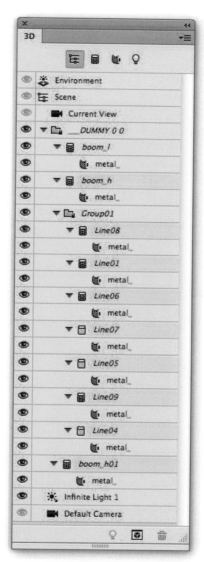

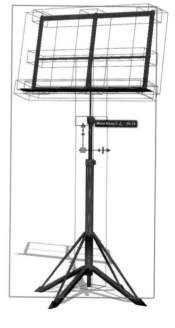

4 We can turn this to our advantage. By clicking on the triangle next to the folder we can pop it open to see its contents: so we can select just *Group01*, for instance, which is the head of the music stand.

This allows us to manipulate it independently; we could, say, rotate it to a different angle if we wish.

5 Here, we want to select the head and the upper shaft, to make the whole music stand shorter. Photoshop doesn't presently let you select a whole group alongside a single 3D layer, so we need to pop open the group and select all the layers inside it – together with the *boom* layers that hold the music shaft.

6 Now, we're able to use the **3D Axis** controller to slide the whole assembly up and down – just as we would with a real music stand.

Models with insides

SOME MODELS ARE CREATED to be taken apart – such as this splendidly detailed anatomical figure, courtesy of Digimation's 3D Archive. We can use Photoshop's Cross Section feature to cut her in half, revealing all the internal organs that were previously hidden. You'll also find car models with this level of internal detail.

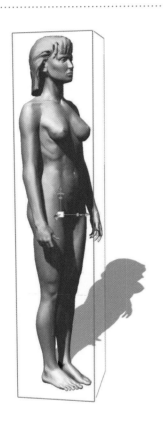

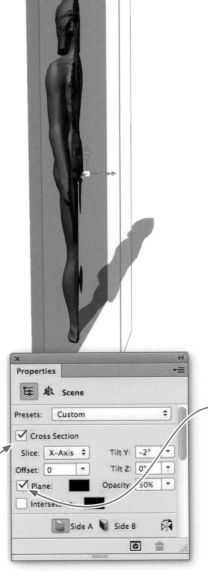

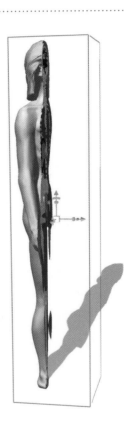

1 You can download this figure from **3DPhotoshop.net**. It's a large and complex model, so be aware that it may take some time for Photoshop to open it.

2 Select the **Scene** option in the **3D panel**, and check the **Cross Section** box in the **Properties panel**. You'll see the figure cut in half down the center.

3 The gray overlay indicates the plane of operation – one side of the plane is visible, the other is hidden.

That plane can be irritating if you don't need it, so you can either reduce its **Opacity** by dragging the slider, or disable it entirely using the **Plane** checkbox.

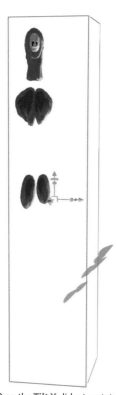

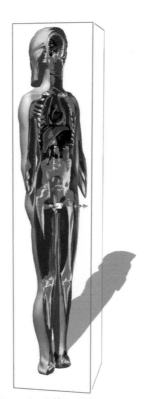

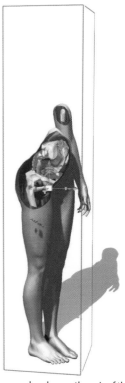

4 Drag the **Tilt Y** slider to rotate the plane of the cross section. As you can see, this has moved it right to the back, so only a small part of the figure is now visible ●

5 Drag the **Offset** slider to move the cross section forward through the figure. You can slide it forward and backward to choose your point of view ●

6 You can also change the axis of the slice. We're been working on the **X-Axis**; here, I've changed to the **Y-Axis** and adjusted the **Tilt X** slider for this angled view ●

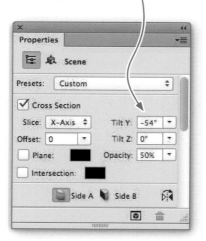

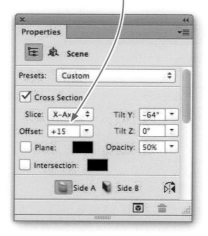

Correcting mismatch errors

3D OBJECTS DOWNLOADED from third-party sources often appear with errors in them – either errors of placement, in which object parts will appear shifted out of position, or (more commonly) errors due to texture failing to show up correctly.

This model is inspired by *Unique Forms of Continuity in Space*, created in 1913 by Umberto Boccioni. Downloaded from archive3d.net, the model shows both of these faults. Fortunately, they're easy to correct.

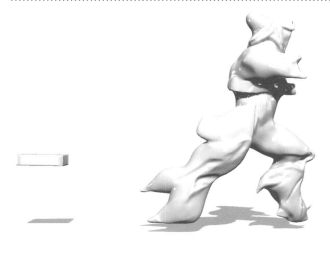

1 Here's the original model, and you can see both problems clearly: the two foot pedestals have come detached and have floated off into space. You can download this model here:

bit.ly/191TIDv

2 When we look at the **3D panel**, we can see that there are three items: a group containing the main sculpture, and separate objects (incorrectly labeled as *Group*) for each of the foot pedestals.

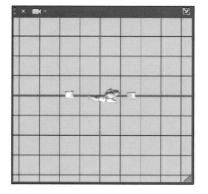

3 At first glance, it appears that the rear pedestal has disappeared behind the sculpture, while the front one is in front and to the right of it.

This is where the **Secondary View** comes in: it's able to show that the pedestals are more or less aligned, but the main shift is vertical rather than left or right.

Note: The Secondary View defaults to a far-off viewpoint. You can zoom in by holding ⌥ *alt* and dragging in the view.

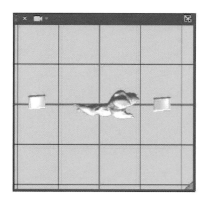

Keyboard shortcuts   (MAC)(WIN)(BOTH)

4 Because the two pedestals appear as separate objects, and helpfully outside the main group, we can select them independently simply by clicking on them with the **Move tool**.

It's now a straightforward matter to drag the frontmost pedestal left and up, so it fits in place beneath the front foot.

Because the object is so small, you'll probably find it easier to use the **3D Axis** controller, rather than dragging on one of the object's faces.

5 Here's the frontmost pedestal moved into place. I've overlapped it with the foot slightly, so the foot is embedded in it – otherwise it would be balancing on a tiny point of contact.

The rear pedestal can now be manipulated in the same way.

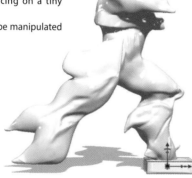

6 With both pedestals now in place, the sculpture is much improved – it's almost back to the state it was in when the designer created it.

It's still missing its textures, though, which is why it's plain white. We'll address that omission on the following pages.

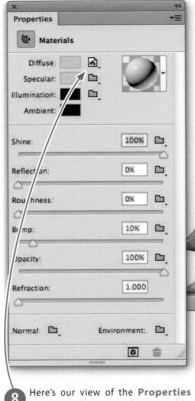

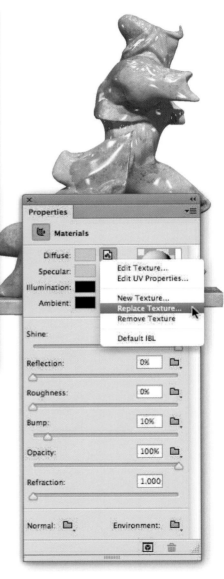

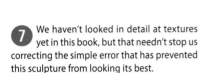

7 We haven't looked in detail at textures yet in this book, but that needn't stop us correcting the simple error that has prevented this sculpture from looking its best.

In the **3D panel**, you'll see that when you pop open each object (confusingly named *Groups*, as we've already observed) there's an item named, helpfully, *Material* beneath it. Click on that name to open the **Materials** pane in the **Properties panel**.

8 Here's our view of the **Properties panel** with the **Materials** pane visible. The texture is the **Diffuse** component, indicated by a tiny icon next to the color swatch at the top of the panel.

To the right of the swatch is a gray ball, which should be showing the texture of the object. It's showing nothing at all; that's because the texture has become detached.

9 Click on the icon next to the **Diffuse** swatch, and choose **Replace Texture** from the pop-up menu. Navigate to the folder that contained the 3D object, and choose **bronze1.jpeg**. The texture will instantly be applied to the model, as seen above.

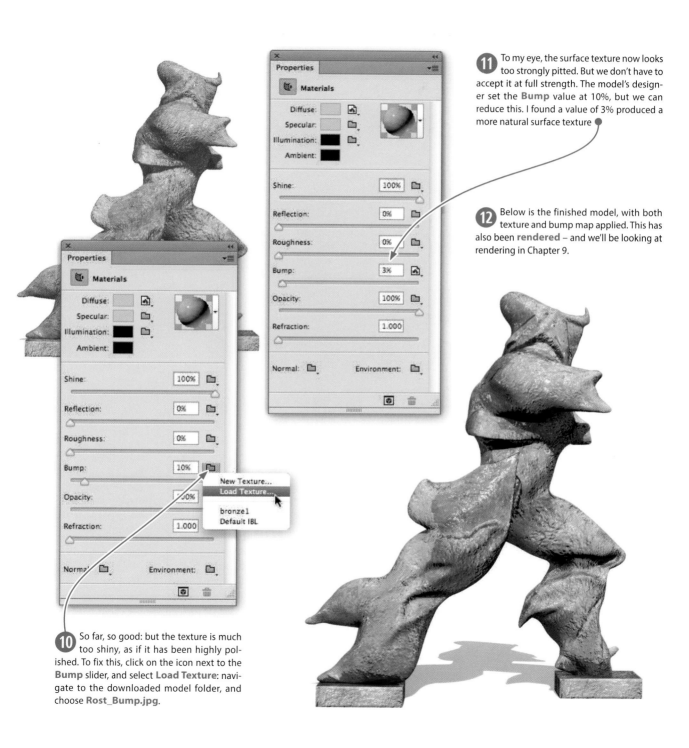

11 To my eye, the surface texture now looks too strongly pitted. But we don't have to accept it at full strength. The model's designer set the **Bump** value at 10%, but we can reduce this. I found a value of 3% produced a more natural surface texture

12 Below is the finished model, with both texture and bump map applied. This has also been **rendered** – and we'll be looking at rendering in Chapter 9.

10 So far, so good: but the texture is much too shiny, as if it has been highly polished. To fix this, click on the icon next to the **Bump** slider, and select **Load Texture**: navigate to the downloaded model folder, and choose **Rost_Bump.jpg**.

When models go bad

YOU'LL FIND A WIDE RANGE of 3D models available for free on the Internet, and some of them are very good indeed. Some, however, fail to open properly in Photoshop. This isn't necessarily a fault with the models themselves, but more a mismatch between the file format they're written in and the format as Photoshop interprets it. Even the familiar .3DS and .OBJ formats are subject to variation, and if you choose a model made with the wrong flavor, you'll be unable to make it work.

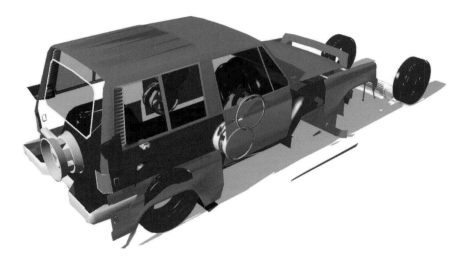

1 This model of a jeep was downloaded from **www.3dm3.com**, a good source of free 3D objects.

But sometimes the objects explode on contact with Photoshop. This jeep, for instance, is composed of a number of 3D objects that have all shifted by a random amount, mainly along the Z-axis: the front tires have shot in front of the vehicle, where the wheels themselves have ended up embedded in the passenger side door.

You could probably reconstruct this jeep by dragging everything back to its proper place, but it's barely worth the considerable effort.

2 Some models have construction mismatches when opened in Photoshop. This model of the Space Shuttle, for instance, is a high-resolution model with textures included downloaded from NASA.

Some of the textures on the model – the windows, the US name and flag on the tail, the wing coloring – are fine; but the texture on the sides, and the nose, have failed to wrap around the model correctly.

It is possible to correct this, by editing the textures as they appear in the **Layers panel** – and they're all named for easy reference – but it's a tricky process to get right.

3 All seems fine with this model of a computer desk, downloaded from **Google 3D Warehouse**. The model was only available in **Sketchup** format, which meant it was necessary to open it in Sketchup and then export it as a **.kmz** (Google Earth) file.

But although the model looked fine with basic preview texturing, when it was rendered the textures all went horribly wrong. And because they were all enclosed within the single Sketchup file, there was no way to fix the problem – other than building all the textures from scratch.

4 On the left, as the label says, is a bust of A. Sevilla. Who is A. Sevilla? He's the guy who scanned his own head and combined the result with a model of a bust he found online, which he then published on 3D print sharing website **thingiverse.com**.

The trouble is, while Mr. Sevilla himself is of reasonable quality, the bust he's chosen as the base is a very low-quality model – it has what 3D modelers call a *low poly count*, which means very few polygons make up the figure. It's important to check that your models are of decent quality to use before spending too much time modifying them.

5 An adorable cherub. No, it isn't, it's a ghastly travesty of renaissance art that doesn't deserve a place on your computer, let alone in Photoshop. Come on, people, there has to be a taste threshold.

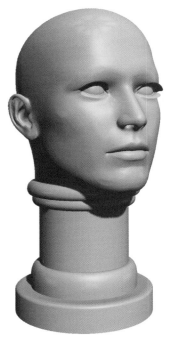

6 I've used this combined figure (head modeled in **Daz Studio**, plinth modeled in Photoshop) in a few places in this book, and wanted to use it to demonstrate textures as well. It wasn't until I applied the glass texture, right, that I realized the problem: as a Daz Studio figure, the head included both eyes and teeth, with a full mouth interior – clearly visible when made of glass.

7 This elephant was downloaded from **Google 3D Warehouse**. As the creator says: "Never making animals again. Too many round shapes." Indeed.

8 This human figure, downloaded from **archive3d.net**, looked fine in the thumbnail. But look at the hands: it's an extremely low-resolution model, which will look like an artificial construct wherever you use it.

Just workable far in the distance, but you do need to check the quality of 3D models before you commit to using them in your Photoshop projects.

PART TWO
Lighting and materials

PART TWO
Lighting and
materials

9 Rendering

PHOTOSHOP IS GREAT at producing 3D visuals, in real time, that move around as you drag the mouse and that can be scaled, turned, twisted and otherwise deformed on the fly. A vast number of calculations go into representing on-screen the detailed models that have been designed or incorporated into whichever 3D scene you happen to be working on.

But while you're working on the image, all you're seeing is a *preview* of the finished scene, and not the final artwork itself. The models tend to look a little like plastic, rather than the metal, fur, fabric or glass that they're supposed to be made of. *Rendering* the scene produces the final high-quality artwork, and there's a big difference between this and the preview you've been looking at.

The trouble is that rendering can take a very long time – hours, in fact. That's why *Toy Story*, the first wholly 3D-modeled movie, was based around toys: if all the main characters are made of plastic, they're going to be that much quicker to render. Several hours may be a long time for a single image, but several hours for each of up to 30 frames per second for a movie lasting an hour and a half is a lot of render time.

1 Some materials, particularly those that are shiny or transparent, are especially hard to make out in the preview. We can see the shape of this juicer, but little more.

2 When the image is rendered we can at last see it as the designer intended. Not only are the materials much clearer, but the whole object now has smooth, anti-aliased edges.

The render process

TO RENDER A MODEL, simply choose Render from the 3D menu. Photoshop will go through several passes to produce the final image, rendering it in chunks. Here's an overview of the process.

1 This is the original construction, in standard preview mode. As you can see, both the lettering and the vase look as if they're made of plastic; we can see clearly where the objects are, but we get little idea of their final appearance.

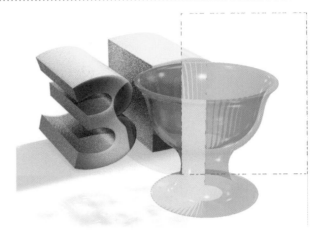

2 When we choose **Render** from the **3D** menu, Photoshop goes through the process of producing the final image. It breaks it up into manageable regions, treating each one individually: here, as you can see, the top-left quarter has had its first render pass, and the lettering is looking much more like metal.

3 With the top-right quarter having had its first render pass as well, we can see how the look is coming on: the glass now correctly refracts the view of the lettering seen through it. Compare this with the bottom of the vase, which has yet to be rendered, and you can clearly see the difference in quality.

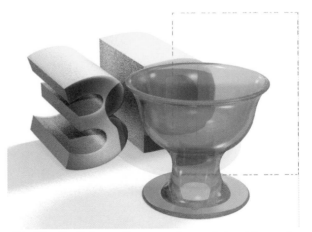

4 After the first pass, the process is repeated and the render becomes more refined. Going over the image in stages like this makes it much easier to check if this is what you want: you get a good idea of how things are going to shape up very quickly. If it isn't right, you can cancel the render at any time by pressing the **esc** key.

5 Rendering is not a quick business. Here, the glass looks almost finished, but the lettering is still composed of many tiny dots. Metal is a complex surface to render effectively.

6 As the render continues, the image gradually becomes more and more refined. It gets to the stage where you can see less and less difference between each pass.

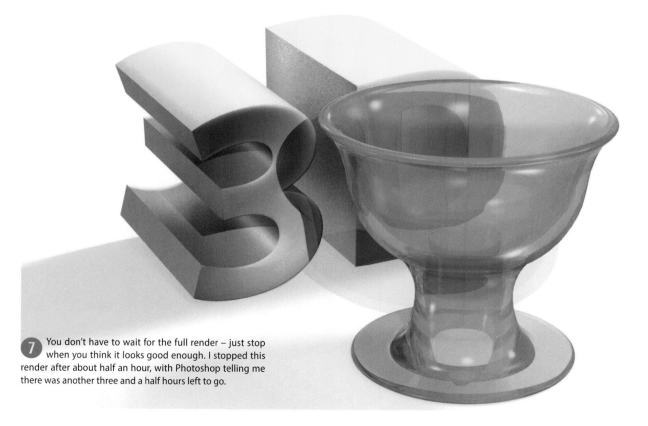

7 You don't have to wait for the full render – just stop when you think it looks good enough. I stopped this render after about half an hour, with Photoshop telling me there was another three and a half hours left to go.

Three kinds of shadow

ONE OF THE MORE CONFUSING aspects of rendering an image in Photoshop is dealing with the shadows. There are three different ways of settings shadows, and it's important to know the difference between them – especially when rendering cutout objects.

1 When you select any single **Light**, you can choose whether or not it casts a shadow – and how soft that shadow is

2 Here's a typical scene, seen in preview mode. The shadow cast by the light looks a little rough, but is otherwise accurate.

4 All that shadow around the edge is set by the **Environment** pane of the **Properties panel**. It's a general ambient shadow, cast not upon (or by) the object but on the scene around it.

When rendering a complete scene it can look very good – and you can use the **Softness** control to smooth it out. It's fairly soft already, though, so you're unlikely to see much difference when changing this value

3 When we **Render** the scene, we find shadow creeping in all around the edges of the image. That can be a problem.

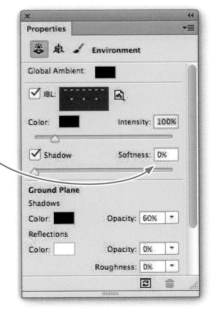

5 When working with cutout objects, as we are in the main in this book, that global ambient shadow is just an annoyance.

If you're producing cutouts with no background, then it's best to turn off the background shadow altogether. You can do so in the **Properties panel** by unchecking the checkbox ●

6 The position and softness of shadows on the ground are both set by the **Light** controls – and we'll look at these in more detail in the next chapter.

But the **Opacity** of the ground shadows is set in the **Environment** pane of the **Properties panel**, along with other ambient settings. Drag the **Opacity** slider to change the strength of the shadow ●

7 You can also turn all the shadows off, using – a little confusingly – the **Scene** pane of the **Properties panel**. Note that this will hide shadows cast by the object, including those cast on itself, but will *not* affect the general shading on the object.

Turn off all these shadows using the checkbox at the bottom of the panel ●

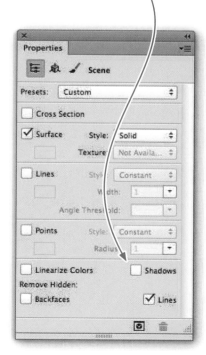
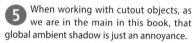

Render modes

AS WELL AS CREATING photorealistic renders, Photoshop has a range of additional ways of rendering your objects, controlled using the Scene pane of the Properties panel. You can customize the way your renders appear to a large degree, or you can start from one of the presets. There are a lot of presets to choose from; here are some of the most interesting.

1 In the **3D panel**, choose the **Scene** option right at the top. This will open the relevant pane in the **Properties panel**.

2 Choose from one of the **Presets** in the pop-up list at the top of the panel, or modify the settings to produce your own variants.
Experiment with the settings to see what difference is made when they're changed. You can't break Photoshop, so tinker at will

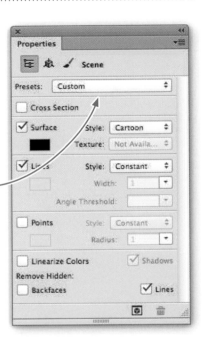

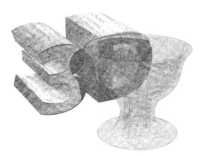

Sketch Scattered: A hand-drawn effect that produces the impression that the models have been drawn with a pencil.

Sketch Thin Pencil: A denser variant on the sketch preset, with strong lines simulating a drawn or engraved image.

Sketch Grass: Another variant on the sketch effect, this one is designed to look as if the image has been drawn in, er, grass.

Wireframe: Shows the underlying structure that makes up the model. Good for creating obviously computer-generated effects.

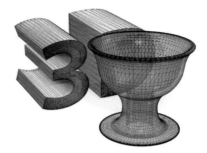

Solid Wireframe: The same wireframe effect, this time overlaid on the original model to produce a composite result.

Shaded Wireframe: Another wireframe effect, in which the wireframe takes on the colors of the original model.

Normals: A colorful representation of the bump mapping effect produced by creating *normals* from an image or texture.

Depth Map: A view of the scene entirely in terms of depth – the closer to the camera, the brighter the result.

Unlit Texture: The scene composed entirely of flat textures. Very good for creating a stark, graphic effect, especially from text.

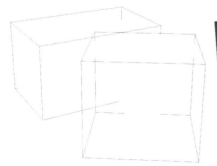

Bounding Box: A way of viewing the scene based purely on the volume each object takes up in the 3D world.

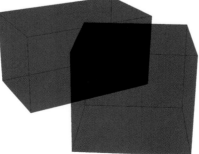

Transparent Bounding Box Outline: A variant on the Bounding Box in which the models are shaded as well as outlined.

Custom: All the presets can be modified at will. Here, I've started with a standard render and added an outline to it.

Depth of field

WHEN RENDERING 3D OBJECTS, everything is in focus – and we can produce crisp, clear images that are even better than photographs. But that's also a problem; in real photography, it's rare to find a scene in which the whole image is in focus.

Photoshop's camera controls include a pair of Depth of Field settings, which allow us to determine just how much of the scene is out of focus – and exactly where that focal point is situated.

1 Here's a model of a wrench, from **archive3d.net** – you can download it from **bit.ly/14Q33eK**.

2 Select **Camera** in the **3D panel**, then switch to the **Properties panel**. The **Depth** setting will be zero; increase it to make part of the image out of focus.

3 Here's how the preview will appear: blocky squares give only the vaguest indication of how the final rendered image is going to look.

4 When the image is rendered, the whole effect becomes much more subtle. You can see there's only a slight loss of focus here, and it's located at the far end of the wrench.

5 For a more dramatic effect, increase the **Depth** amount. Here, it's set to a value of 6 – and as this rendered view shows, the far end of the wrench is now much more out of focus than the near end.

6 You can control the position at which the wrench is in focus by changing the **Distance** setting. As you drag left and right on the word, you'll see the sharp region moving up and down the wrench.

7 Once the scene is rendered, you can clearly see how the front end of the wrench is now out of focus, whereas the back is crisp and clear.

Although the preview mode doesn't give you much idea of the final appearance of the object, it does allow you to see with some precision where the focal point will lie.

Partial renders

YOU DON'T NEED TO WAIT for a scene to render in its entirety. You can cancel a render at any time by pressing the **esc** key, either because you want to make changes or because you think the quality is good enough for the purpose.

You can also render just a portion of a scene if you want to check how it's going to work out, simply by selecting it with the Marquee tool before rendering.

1 This enlarged view shows a 3D object in standard preview mode. You can clearly see how rough both the edges and the shadows are.

2 The same model after the first render pass. The model itself is smooth, but the shadow is still clearly composed of an array of tiny dots.

3 With the full render complete, you can see how smooth the shadow now is. You can choose at what point a render is good enough and then cancel it.

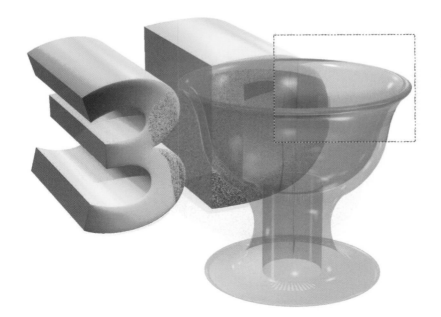

4 Large and complex scenes can take a very long time to render. Here, we only want to check the transparency effect on the vase, and the amount of refraction produced on the lettering beneath.

By making a selection first with the **Rectangular Marquee tool**, we're able to render just that section of the artwork without having to wait for the full thing.

You can create multiple selections and render them all simultaneously, but this will take much longer.

10 Lighting

BUILDING 3D MODELS, or acquiring them from online sources, is just the first part of the process of creating a 3D scene. The next important step is getting the lighting right.

If you want to create a standalone object, such as the bust of Julius Caesar below, then the way you arrange the lighting can completely change the way viewers perceive the image. Plain? Sinister? Scary? Mysterious? All these emotional values can be appended to the object via the use of lighting alone, so it really pays to take the time to think about what you want.

If you're placing an object within an existing scene, then getting the lighting right is essential to making the item look as if it really belongs there. Often, it's simply a matter of dragging the light to the position you want it; sometimes, you need to balance several different factors in order to make the lighting work.

Basic lighting controls

1 Here's our version of Bocchioni's *Unique Forms of Continuity in Space*, as featured in the previous chapter. You can download it from **bit.ly/191TIDv.**

2 When we turn the world view around (not just the model, but the whole scene), the lights move with it. So when we're looking at the rear of the model, the lights are behind it.

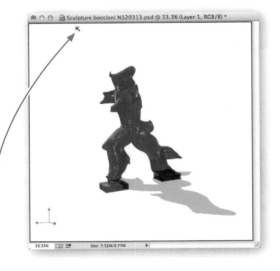

3 To access the lights, click on the small light icon toward the edge of the Photoshop window. Note that if you're zoomed out, it may appear in the gray area outside the canvas.

4 Clicking on the light icon brings the lighting controller into view. It's this controller that allows us to set the direction of the lighting directly on the image.

5 The pin indicates the direction the light is coming from; but you can drag on the lighting sphere to spin it around. Here, I've lit the figure from the front.

6 Lighting can be from any angle you like. In this instance, the figure is lit from below: you can see the shadows of the arm cast onto the head.

7 Another way to access the lighting control is to hold *Shift* and click on any visible part of the shadow. This can be a quicker method than finding the icon.

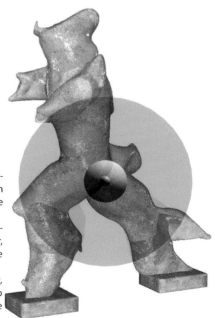

9 The **Move to view** button is at the bottom of the **Properties panel**. When clicked, it moves the light so it's directly in line with the current view of the object.

This button is especially useful when building or importing models, as it provides a clear, mainly shadow-free view of the object you're working on.

It's never a good option for a final view, though, and you'll almost certainly want to move the lighting direction elsewhere before you **Render** the scene.

8 When a light is selected, the **Properties panel** will change to show the lighting controls. Here you can choose a **Preset**, change the **Type** of light, and vary the **Intensity** and the **Shadow** softness. We'll look at all of these factors in this chapter.

Working with multiple lights

ALL THE MODELS we've looked at so far have used just one light source. But in real life, this often isn't the case: you might have light from a desk lamp, but there will also be ambient light from a window.

Photoshop allows you to add several lights, of different kinds, and to position them as you choose. You can also work with colored lights to create dramatic special effects, producing a very theatrical appearance.

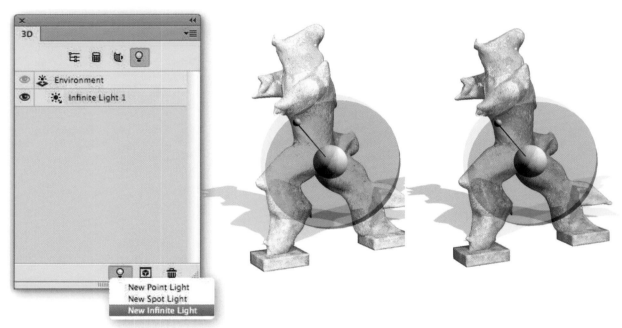

1 You can make extra lights for your scene by clicking the **Light** icon at the bottom of the **3D panel**.

From the pop-up menu, choose between the three types of light available. You'll generally want to use an **Infinite** Light, as this provides the sort of light generated by a far-off source, such as the sun.

You can also use the **3D panel** to delete lights you don't want, by dragging them to the Trash icon at the bottom.

2 When you add an extra light it appears in the default North-West position, illuminating the scene. You can see the extra shadow cast on the ground behind the figure.

3 It's likely that when you create a new light, the whole scene will now be too bright. You can fix this by reducing the **Intensity** of the light: either click in the number field and type a new number or, better, drag left and right on the word *Intensity* itself to change the value ●

A splash of color

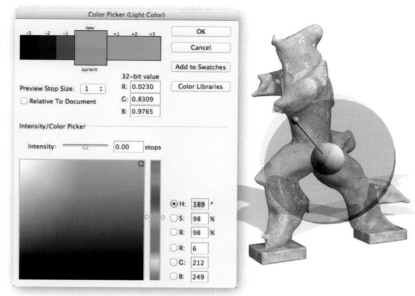

4 The most dramatic results can be had from changing the color of the new light. Click the **Color** swatch in the **Properties panel** to open the **Color Picker**.

5 Choose a color range from the vertical rainbow gradient. If you prefer, use either the **HSB** or the **RGB** fields to refine the color numerically.

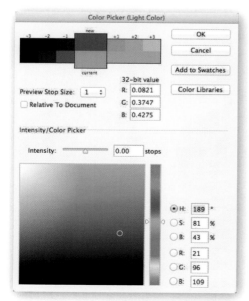

6 When using the **Color Picker** in everyday Photoshop activity, you'd drag up and down, and left and right, in the large square to the left of the rainbow gradient to change the brightness and saturation.

But as we're now working with light, reducing the brightness of the color will simply result in less of that light on the object, as can be seen on the right.

It's better to leave the saturation and brightness at their maximum value, and to adjust the intensity of each light in the **Properties panel** instead.

Lighting presets

AT THE TOP of the Properties panel, when a light is selected, you'll find the presets pop-up. This enables quick access to a set of lighting setups, many of them using multiple lights, that you can quickly apply to your scenes. Of course, once you've selected one, you can then fine-tune each light individually if you wish.

Photoshop ships with15 lighting presets; here they are for easy reference.

| Blue | CAD Optimized | Cold | Dawn |

| Lush | Mardi Gras | Night Lights | Primary Colors |

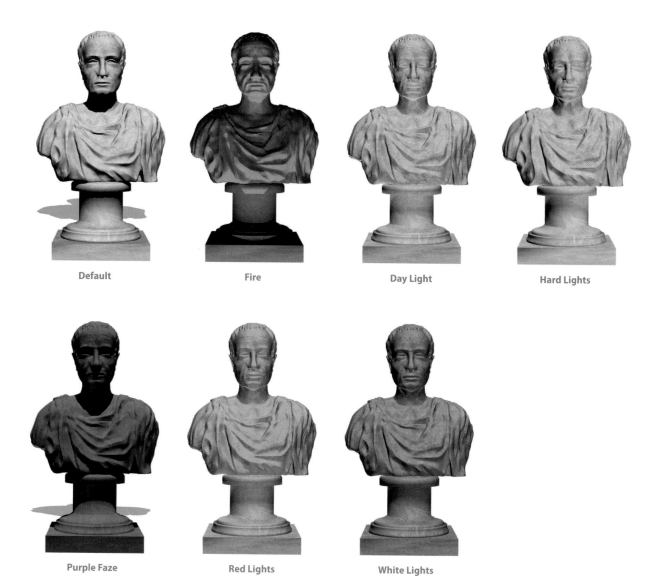

Default

Fire

Day Light

Hard Lights

Purple Faze

Red Lights

White Lights

Point lights

POINT LIGHTS are lights that are positioned at a visible location within the scene. They're used for placing lights inside lamps, on candles, inside cars – anywhere where you want the light source itself to be visible.

We'll look at placing lights inside objects later in the book. For now, let's stick with our sculpture and see how changing the light type to Point affects the artwork.

1 When you change a light type from **Infinite** to **Point** you'll probably find that you can hardly see the light at all; in addition, when you select it, you'll see two wireframe spheres around it, one of which will almost certainly extend far off the edge of your canvas.

The reason for this is that **Point** lights need to be positioned very differently than other forms of lights. By default, lights are located way off in the distance; but **Point** lights need to be moved much closer to the action.

Clicking the **Move to view** button at the bottom of the **Properties panel** will move the light so you can see it more clearly ●

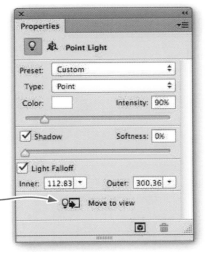

2 You can move a **Point** light into the scene by holding ⌥ *alt* and clicking on the place where you want it to appear.

It's quite likely that when you do this the light will end up embedded inside your object, so you'll need to move it away. Use the 3D Axis controller to move the light in each direction until you get it exactly where you want it.

3 If you look at the **Properties panel**, you'll see that the light now includes extra controls that weren't there before. We'll look at those next.

4 The **Falloff** controls at the bottom of the panel determine the spread of the light. Here, the **Inner** and **Outer** values are almost identical, which produces a very sharp boundary between the lit and the unlit areas.

The **Falloff** values correspond to the inner and outer rings of the wireframe sphere, as seen on the model (I've rendered the scene here to show the lighting effect more clearly).

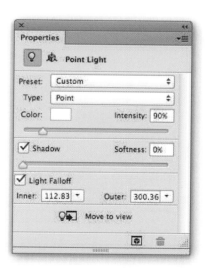

5 Setting a larger **Outer** Falloff value allows the light to spill further in the scene. You can see here how doubling the value enables the light to hit the pedestal and lower legs of the sculpture. In addition, we can now see the shadow on the ground.

If the value were increased to its maximum, the shadow would extend all the way to the horizon.

Spot lights

SPOT LIGHTS cast light in a cone, as the name implies. They're also useful for creating such effects as car headlamps, flashlight beams, and so on. Like Point lights, they have their own set of controls, both within the panel and directly on the model.

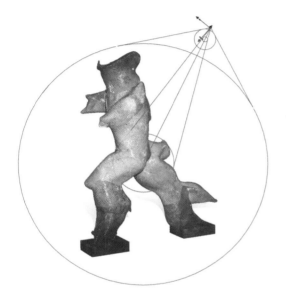

1 Start by choosing **Spot** as the light type from the pop-up menu at the top of the **Properties panel**.

You may well find that the light appears to disappear, since it will take on the position of the previous light placement. As with the **Point** light, you can hold ⌥ *ctrl* and click on the image to set the direction toward which the light points.

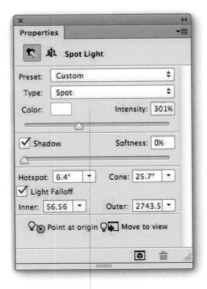

2 As well as the Inner and Outer **Falloff** controls that we looked at on the previous page, there are two new controls here: **Hotspot** and **Cone**.

Changing the **Cone** value affects the side of the light cast upon the object, as can be seen above. Set the value by dragging on the word *Cone*, or by clicking on the arrow next to the number field and dragging the slider.

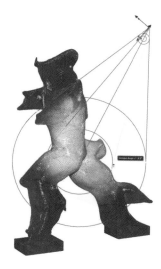

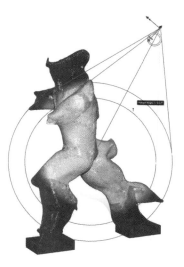

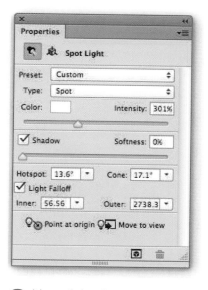

3 The **Hotspot** angle determines the bright point in the middle of the cone. As well as setting this numerically, you can click near the inner circle, and drag up and down to change the settings.

4 If you drag beyond the **Cone** size, then that will also be increased to make room for the increased **Hotspot** size.

5 It's worth keeping an eye on the **Properties panel** to see just how the changes you make by dragging affect the numbers. It can help you to see what's going on in the image.

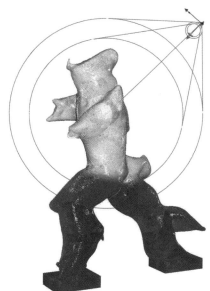

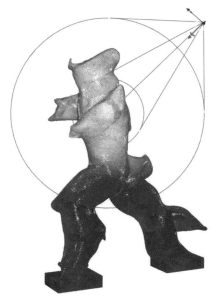

6 When the **Hotspot** size is very close to the **Cone** size, you'll see a sharp cutoff between the lit and unlit areas. This can look very artificial if you aren't careful.

7 It's often better to reduce the **Hotspot** size a little way, so that there's a smoother transition between the light and shade regions in the scene.

Shadows

SHADOWS ARE AN ESSENTIAL part of lighting. They give objects definition, substance and location: they indicate exactly how an object fits into its surroundings. Here, we'll take a look at the basics of creating shadows along with your lighting. You can download this car at **bit.ly/13BLJer**.

1 When an object has no shadows, it appears strangely detached from reality. Even though this is a cutout, it appears to be disconnected from the page.

2 Adding a shadow immediately gives the object a sense of belonging in its environment, even if that environment happens to be a white space extending off into infinity.

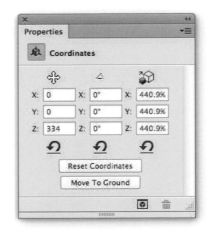

3 Once you start introducing shadows, you have to be concerned with how an object sits on the **Ground Plane**. Here, the car is clearly a little way off the ground. When the shadow is added, it makes the car appear to be floating.

That may, of course, be the effect you want to produce, and it can be a very effective way of showing that an object is flying.

4 Just in case you don't want to depict a flying car, there's an easy way to place it back on the ground. Open the **Properties panel** and, with the **Mesh** selected, you'll see this view. Check that the angles of rotation are set to zero, and then hit the **Move To Ground** button. This will place the car securely on terra firma.

If the object has been rotated in multiple dimensions, click the **Reset Coordinates** button to move it back to the origin.

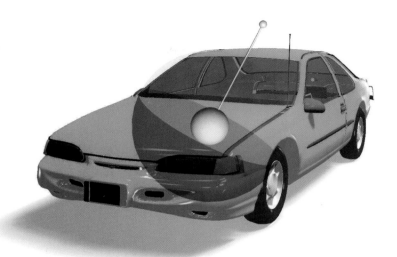

5 Shadows are enabled in Photoshop by default: if you don't want them, uncheck the **Shadow** box in the **Properties panel**.

Shadows first appear hard-edged, as seen so far in this book. But you can soften them, by dragging the **Softness** slider.

When you're working with objects, you see a preview in which the shadow is shown with a fuzzy, dotted edge, as seen above right; but when the model has been **rendered**, that shadow regains its full softness, as seen lower right here.

6 When multiple lights are applied, each light will cast its own shadow.

You can choose to turn the shadow on and off for each of the lights, and you can set a different degree of softness for each light as well.

Special effects with shadows

AS WELL AS ADDING emphasis and grounding to objects, shadows can play a much more important role: in special instances they can themselves become the artwork. Here, we'll look at how to take ordinary text and turn it into something beautiful.

1 This text is set in Myriad Bold Condensed, and has been extruded to make a 3D object as we saw at the beginning of the book. The text is set in white; with the light behind it, the face of the text itself is strongly in shadow.

2 When we move the light to the front, the shadow appears behind it – and the light is so strong that the text itself has become entirely bleached out. From this position, we can just make out the wording, although it's hard to discern the shadow.

3 When we spin the world view around to view the scene from above, we get something rather splendid: the text is still just about legible, but its meaning is made much clearer by that long, elongated shadow stretching out behind it.

11 Placing materials

SO FAR, WE'VE LOOKED at creating and lighting 3D models. But all our models look as if they're made of plastic; they may be the right shape, but they have no texture to them. The exception is the Boccioni sculpture we worked with in Chapter 8, which came with a basic marble texture.

There's a lot more to texture than just placing a pattern on top of an object: many different factors affect how the surface of a 3D object is displayed. For this reason, textures are referred to in Photoshop as *materials*, since they include surface properties as well as simple patterns.

To start this chapter, we'll take an existing 3D object whose textures have gone astray on the way between 3DS Max and Photoshop, and see what happens when we replace them one by one. The model is taken from the extensive archive3D.net website, and can be downloaded from **bit.ly/10c5YB5**.

1 Here's the plant as it appears in Photoshop. There's clearly some modeling on the leaves, as they're reflecting the light in a way that suggests a bumpy surface; but there's no texture here. A glance at the **3D panel** reveals that textures are expected, but sadly they all appear to be missing from this model.

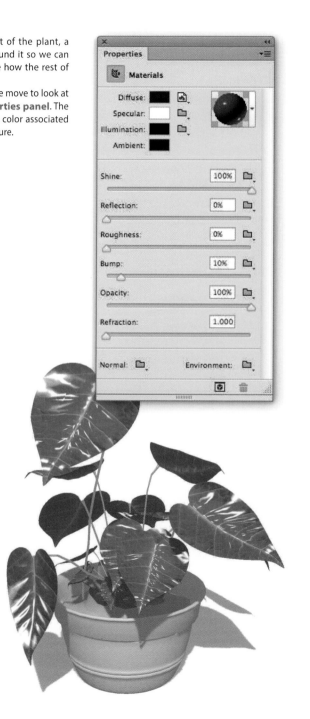

2 When we click on any part of the plant, a bounding box appears around it so we can move it independently (and note how the rest of the object is dimmed slightly).

When we click a *second* time, we move to look at the **Materials** pane in the **Properties panel**. The preview ball shows that there is a color associated with the leaves, but no texture.

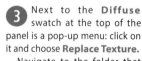

3 Next to the **Diffuse** swatch at the top of the panel is a pop-up menu: click on it and choose **Replace Texture.**

Navigate to the folder that contains the plant object you downloaded, and in that folder you'll find a range of additional files. The task now is to match those files with the parts of the plant to which they should be attached.

Fortunately, they're reasonably well labeled. So when we find a file named *arch41_019_leaf.jpg*, we can assume it's the texture for the leaves. Click OK to load it up, and you can see the difference when it's mapped onto the leaves.

4 By looking at the other files in the folder we can make a fair guess as to where they belong in the model.

For instance, there's a file named *Leaf01_bump.tga*. This tells us that it's a **Bump** texture, and so should be loaded accordingly.

Bump textures are black and white channels that allow Photoshop to simulate height and depth on surfaces. They give the impression of surface texture without requiring complex modeling.

To the right of the word **Bump** in the **Properties panel**, you'll see a small folder. Click on it, and choose **Load Texture**. Navigate to the *Leaf01_bump.tga* file, and click OK to load it.

Here's the result: shiny, more textural-looking leaves.

5 Also in the folder is a file named *Leaf01_specular.tga*. The **specularity** of a 3D object controls the degree to which it reflects the light upon it.

You can see from the thumbnail on the left that this is a mainly dark image, with faint highlights picked out along the shape of the leaves. This means that the lighting will be greatly dulled down, except for a slight shine over the leaf area.

We can apply this texture in the same way as before, first clicking on the folder icon to the right of the word **Specular** at the top of the **Properties panel**.

When it's applied, you can see how that very brash lighting has been dulled down by a considerable degree.

6 The naming procedure isn't always so easy to guess. There's a file in the folder named *Leaf01_alpha.tga* – but where should we apply it?

Looking at the file helps. It shows a clear leaf shape, with the veins highlighted. I'm guessing this should determine the level of illumination on the plant leaves.

To apply it, click on the folder next to the **Illumination** icon near the top of the **Properties panel**, and choose this file from the folder structure.

When it's applied, you can see how it brings back a lot of the detail that appeared to have been lost from the leaves: the veins now stand out much more clearly.

7 There's also a file in the folder named *ground.jpg*. Well, it's fairly obvious from the name alone where this should go; and when we preview the image, it's clear that it shows a section of lumpy earth.

Select the earth within the 3D model, and follow the same procedure we've been using all along to add this texture as the **Diffuse** property of the object.

There are, in fact, two separate objects that make up the earth in this model, and it's worth selecting both of them and applying the texture to them each. This has to be done one at a time, as they're separate objects.

8 There was one texture in the folder that I couldn't easily place: it's called *Shammy 2.jpeg*. It may well be that this was intended for the stalks. But just for good measure, I applied it to the pot, since that was conspicuously lacking in texture.

Apply this texture (assuming you agree with me that this is where it goes; you may well not) in the usual way.

With all the textures now in place, the plant is restored to the state in which its creator intended it to be viewed.

9 Here's the finished plant, with additional lighting added and rendered to produce the finished artwork. It's a convincing and detailed object, which would blend well into any 3D scene.

Compare it with the image we started with, which had no texture at all, and I'm sure you'll agree it's a huge improvement.

Coloring 3D objects

WHEN WE CREATE a 3D object, it comes into the world devoid of materials. The simplest way to prevent that gray feeling is to change the object's color.

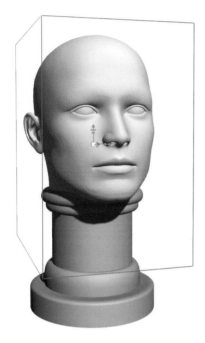

1 This is the head, modeled in Daz Studio, that we looked at briefly in Chapter 8. You can download the 3D model from **3DPhotoshop.net**.

When you click on it, you'll see that the head and the plinth are two separate objects: just the head is selected here.

2 Click a second time on the head and the **Properties panel** will reveal the **Materials** pane. The **Diffuse** texture is what we're going to change here; click on the swatch next to the name to open the **Color Picker**, to choose a new color for the head ●

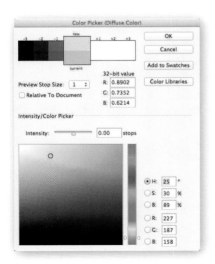

3 When the **Color Picker** opens, you can first select a color from the rainbow strip, then click within the large square to refine the color selection. The saturation is graduated from left to right, and the brightness from top to bottom.

As you click in the **Color Picker**, you'll see the color changing on the head in real time.

Creating a material from scratch

SELECTING A COLOR for an object is all very well, but color on its own tends to make objects look as if they're made of plastic. Instead, let's apply the same color by creating a new texture.

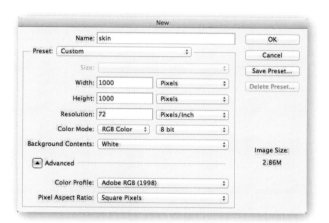

1 Rather than clicking on the color swatch next to the **Diffuse** name in the **Properties panel**, click the icon to the right of it. From the pop-up menu, choose **New Texture** and the dialog above will appear. A size of 1000 pixels square is a good starting point.

2 When the new texture is created, two rather odd things will happen. First, the head will turn pure white, as any existing color applied to it is removed; and second, nothing else will happen.

This is odd because you'd expect the new texture to open in a window. It doesn't; instead, you have to choose **Edit Texture** from the same pop-up menu as before.

3 When the new texture window opens, it will be completely blank. To fill it with color, first select the color you want, either in the **Swatches panel** or the **Color panel**. Then use the keystrokes ⌥ Backspace alt Backspace to fill the area with that color.

When you **Save** the document, the head will be filled with that color.

So far, this is nothing special; but continue overleaf to see how we can begin to build on this process.

Keys   MAC WIN BOTH

Painting on 3D objects

IT MAY SEEM SURPRISING, but Photoshop allows you to paint directly onto 3D objects – using any of the standard painting tools. Here's how it's done.

1 Choose the **Brush tool** and pick a bright blue color. When you paint on the head, the paint will appear exactly as you'd expect, covering the visible part of the head precisely where you paint.

2 That's a little too strong, so **Undo** that painting action and let's try again.
Set the mode of the **Brush tool** to **Multiply**, and choose an **Opacity** of around 20%. Now, when you paint on the head, it's an altogether more subtle effect.

3 Continue to paint on the head, adding a little orange blush for the cheeks and some red for the lips. Stick with the low opacity, and build up the effect in stages.

After applying the beard area you may want to change the mode of the **Brush tool** from **Multiply** to **Normal**, so that the paint doesn't just darken the beard.

If you take a look at the texture window, you'll see everything you've painted opened out and spread across the window.

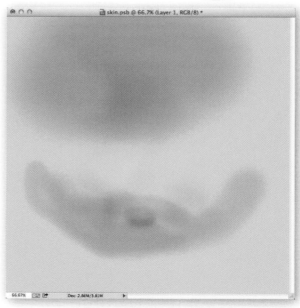

4 The next surprising fact is that you can also paint on the texture window, and the model itself will be updated *in real time* as you paint.

Try painting a scar across the cheek, as I've done here. When you move the brush over the texture window, you'll see a helpful crosshair appear on the model to show where the painting will take place.

If you're not sure about the scar, then create a new layer inside the texture window and paint it on there. Textures, like regular Photoshop files, can hold multiple layers.

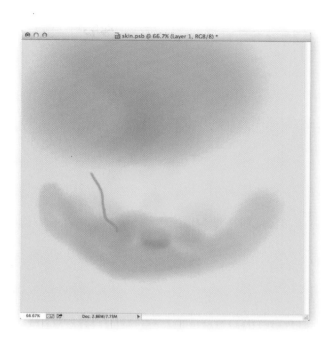

5 You can even add text as part of the texture. Switch to the **Text tool**, and create your text in the font of your choice.

You'll find you need to use **Free Transform** to align and size the text, as it can take a while to find the right location for it.

The text will be created as a separate, editable layer, of course, and so can be moved around and changed at will.

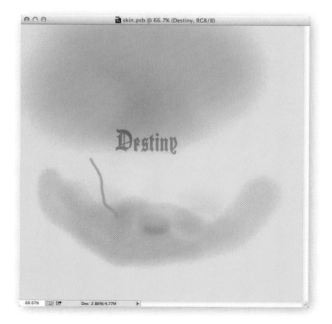

Applying a photographic material

WE'VE LOOKED AT CREATING textures from scratch, but of course any photographic source can also be used as a material. The Internet is awash with sources of textures of all kinds; here, we'll use a couple of texture images that I've photographed.

1 Click twice on the head to open the **Materials** pane of the **Properties panel**, as before.

This time, rather than creating a new texture, choose **Replace Texture** from the pop-up menu to the right of the **Diffuse** item, at the top of the panel.

If you want to load this piece of wood texture, you'll find it on the **3DPhotoshop.net** website. When you open the file, you'll see it applied immediately to the head.

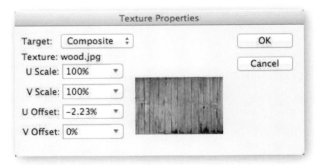

2 The texture can be modified when it's in place: choose **Texture Properties** from the pop-up menu next to the **Diffuse** item at the top of the **Properties panel**. Here, I've offset the texture by -2.23% to make the crack between the wood planks line up with the nose.

3 While you're editing the texture, you'll see some ghostly shapes appearing around the eyes. These are the eyelashes, which were created in Daz Studio and which we can't now get rid of.

They'll disappear as soon as the Texture controls are no longer selected.

4 Let's now go ahead and apply some texture to the plinth. You can choose any texture you like, or experiment with a variety of them; you can download my brick wall from **3DPhotoshop.net**. Once it has been selected, you'll see it applied to the plinth.

Note how, when the plinth is selected, the head is dimmed out to show it's not part of the current selection.

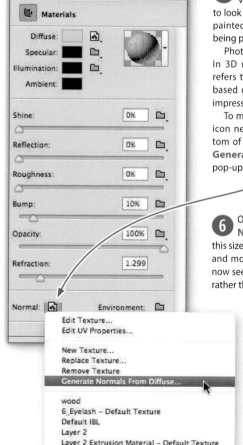

5 Applying a texture to an object is all very well, but they do have a tendency to look a little flat – as if the texture has been painted onto the surface, rather than really being part of the object.

Photoshop has a way of dealing with this. In 3D modeling terms, the word *Normals* refers to a way of making a **bump** texture based on apparent distance. This gives the impression of increased surface depth.

To make this process happen, click on the icon next to the word **Normal** at the bottom of the **Properties panel**, and choose **Generate Normals From Diffuse** from the pop-up menu

6 On the right is the figure with the **Normals** applied. You can see, even at this size, that the texture is now much rougher and more tactile in appearance: the surface now seems to be much more pitted with age, rather than just painted to look that way.

Applying preset materials

PHOTOSHOP COMES WITH a range of preset materials built in, which you can apply directly to your models just by clicking on them. We'll see here how the materials work, and how the different kinds of textures affect the appearance of your scene.

1 Start by selecting the texture in the **Materials** pane of the **3D panel**. There's no bevel or inflation in this object – we just want the *Extrusion Material*.

2 The **Properties panel** will now show the **Materials**. We've looked at this before. At the top right of the panel is a thumbnail showing the current texture placed on a ball. At present, there's no texture applied to this object. Click on the ball to proceed ●

3 When you click on the thumbnail the **Materials presets** pane will open.
Click on any of the presets to apply the texture to your object; if you hover over them without clicking, after a second or two the name of the material will appear ●

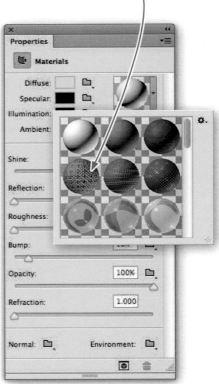

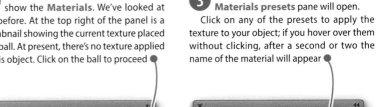

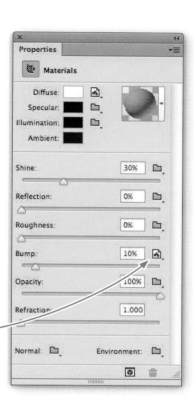

4 Many of the materials contain more than just a surface texture. Here, for example, is the *Fabric Denim* material.

It features a strong diagonal blue stripe, as you can see. But there's more to it than that: there's clearly a lumpiness to the surface here that gives it extra definition.

This is the **Bump** component of the material. You can tell it's there in the **Properties panel**, because the **Bump** control now shows an icon indicating a texture is present; previously, this showed a folder icon ●

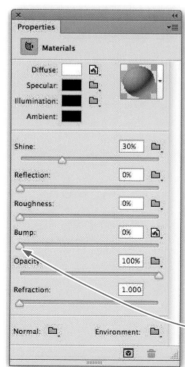

5 We can see how the **Bump** component affects the appearance. Drag the **Bump** slider to 0%, and you can see how flat the goblet now looks.

6 The first material preset in the list, *Fabric Cotton*, is just the *Fabric Denim* material without the diffuse texture: in other words, it just contains the bump map.

Material presets

WE SAW ON THE PREVIOUS PAGE how to apply presets to models. There's a range of built-in presets to choose from, and you can also download more from the pop-up menu in the Properties panel. Here are just some of the available presets, with explanatory notes.

Fabric Leather: A deep, monochromatic leather texture – you'll probably want to brighten the lights when using this one.

Tiles Checkerboard: A black and white pattern that's especially good for seeing just how textures are distorted across the surface.

Organic Orange Peel: But only because its default color is orange. Change the color to gray, and it makes great concrete.

Fun Textured 1: A material that combines a pattern of light and dark with a bump map that matches it, exaggerating the effect.

Fun Textured 2: This texture only uses a bump map – there's no diffuse pattern associated with it.

Fun Textured 3: No pattern, no bump map – but the transparency map makes it full of holes. We'll look at transparency soon.

Gemstone Emerald: There are several glass materials, and they all look meaningless when seen in preview mode.

Gemstone Emerald: It's not until you render the glass materials that you really get any idea of how they're going to look.

Glass (Crystal): The very low opacity (2%) makes this almost invisible, until it's placed on a background (see next section).

Stone Granite: A deep, flecked material. You'll generally want to mix this with other materials, rather than using it on its own.

Stone Marble: This can glare easily, so watch the brightness of your lights when using this one. Best to tone it down a little.

Metal (Brass): All the metallic materials look like plastic until they're rendered in a scene, with a background to reflect.

Plastic Glossy (Blue): A basic highly reflective surface. Because there's no Diffuse texture, it's easy to change the color.

Plastic Matte (Blue): A toned-down version of the previous material. Again, the color can be set to anything you want.

Plastic Textured (Blue): But you have to look very hard to see the texture – it's very subtly applied.

Wood Ash: A highly textured, detailed material that only resembles wood if you're never seen the stuff.

Wood Balsa: A very lightly textured surface that has a faint patterned surface. A very subtle wood effect.

Wood Redwood: Well, it's certainly red, although it doesn't have a particularly woody look. What does Adobe have against wood?

Material surface properties

1 With no shine and no reflection, objects appear dull and lifeless – as if they're made of clay.

2 The **Shine** component adds gloss to the surface. It does so by making the whole surface *darker*, except for the shiny areas. Here, the **Shine** value is set to 50%.

3 When the **Shine** amount is increased to 100%, the highlight spots are reduced in size – because they're not so diffused over the object's surface.

4 **Reflection** differs from **Shine** in that it controls the amount to which an object bounces back ambient light, as well as points of light. The **Reflection** here is set to 50%, producing this strong gloss appearance.

5 When we increase the **Reflection** amount to 100% it makes the whole object brighter, with a resulting loss of detail in the shiny areas.

6 Both Shine and Reflection can have **Textures** associated with them. The texture used here for **Reflection** is half black, half white (left). The black half removes the reflection from that area.

7 The **Roughness** setting controls how the surface diffuses, or blurs, the light that's bouncing off it. Here, the **Reflection** is set to 50%, with the **Roughness** set to 0.

8 When the **Roughness** is increased to just 50%, we see no difference – but when it's increased to 75%, as it is here, we can see the reflected lights blurring a little.

9 Increasing the **Roughness** setting to 100% produces reflections that are so blurred that they're barely visible in the surface material.

10 The **Bump** setting produces the illusion of surface texture. After creating a new texture, I applied the **Clouds** filter for this effect (right). Here it's seen at just 10% strength.

11 Increasing the **Bump** amount to 50% produces a much stronger version of the same effect. The surface now appears much more lumpy.

12 Note that the **Bump** gives only the impression of surface texture. Even when the value is increased to 100%, as it is here, the surface seems very lumpy – but look at the edges: they remain perfectly smooth, with no sign of lumpiness.

Material limitations

PHOTOSHOP'S MATERIALS CONTROLS offer a wide and extensive set of parameters for determining just about every aspect of a material's reflection, refraction, opacity, and much more. But there are some things you can't make a material do. Here are some examples of how not to use them.

1 This application of the **Fun Textured** material works well on the face of the lettering. But when the same material is applied to the extruded sides, it's stretched out of proportion: what looks fine in one place will often look ridiculous in another.

2 The **Fabric Denim** material applied to this frog has wrapped reasonably well around the body, and even works on such fine detail as the fingers (or are they toes?).

But when the same material hits the mouth area, it's clearly stretched out of shape. The original model came with separate textures for these areas; applying the same texture to the whole thing can look wrong.

3 The **Tiles Checkerboard** texture on this head works well over the head itself, accentuating the shape and providing a stark graphic image.

The eyes and eyelashes, though, were exported from Daz Studio as part of the model, and the texture is resized on these areas. Because it has come into Photoshop as a single object, there's no way to separate the eyes and apply a different version of the texture to them; we'd have to choose a pattern-free material to use here.

4 When an object is created by revolving a shape around an axis, there's always a join between the start and finish – and it's especially noticeable with transparent materials. The solution is to select the **Inflation Material** and set its **Opacity** to zero.

5 Some textures just don't work with some surfaces. The bricks are going the wrong way here – they should of course be horizontal rather than vertical. Editing this texture it tricky and time-consuming, but it is just about possible.

6 The polished granite surface works well on this glass, which has now become a stone chalice. But it's compressed on the stem, where it looks artificial. But see page 152 on for a way around this problem.

7 This car model came complete with all the textures it required. Changing them all to a plain, flat texture, such as this blue gloss, produces an effective result.

8 We wouldn't expect to wrap a pattern around the car – that would distort too badly – but we would expect a gold material to work. But look how it distorts over the surface: it's just too complex a shape.

Applying multiple textures

ALL THE OBJECTS we've looked at so far in this chapter have a single surface to which we can apply texture. But when we create objects ourselves in Photoshop, they often have multiple surfaces that are the result of their being built from extruded shapes.

You'll recognize this object – it's the 3D object we created right at the beginning of this book. Here, I've added a round bevel to it. The object now has five distinct surfaces: the front inflation, bevel and extrusion materials, and the back equivalents of the bevel and inflation materials.

1 When you click on a part of the object, you'll first open the **Mesh** pane in the **3D panel**; clicking again will open the **Texture** pane. You can see here how only the *Front Inflation Material* is selected.

2 As each element is selected, the remaining textures in the model are dimmed out to make it clearer where the active selection is located. Here, the *Front Bevel Material* is selected, and the rest is dimmed out.

3 This dimming process makes it easier to see what's going on. But if different textures are applied it can still be hard to tell; it's always worth checking the **3D panel** just to make sure you're using the right surface.

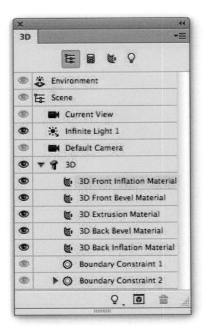

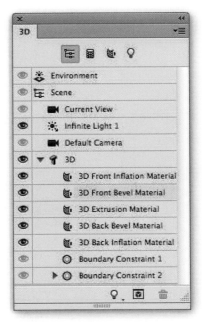

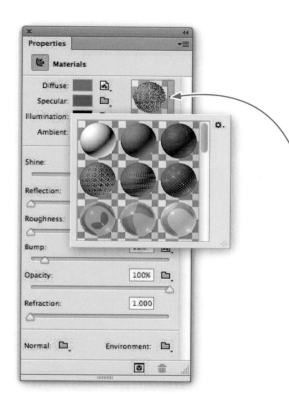

4 You can choose one of the preset materials by opening the **Properties panel** and clicking on the preview ball, then selecting a texture from the pop-up menu. You'll often find, though, that the texture is applied to just a single part of the object.

5 Having all the parts of the model separate in this way means we can apply different textures to each part, and this can result in rich, complex objects such as the one shown above.

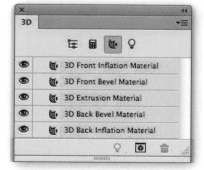

6 Of course, it's likely that you'll want to apply the same texture to the entire object. No need to set each one separately: all you have to do is select all the Material parts in the **3D panel**, and then whichever texture you choose will be applied to them all at the same time.

Editing materials in placed objects

WHEN 3D MODELS ARE DESIGNED outside Photoshop, they frequently come with multiple materials applied to different sections of the model. Each material can be opened and edited individually; here's how to identify and modify different parts of a placed model. You can download this cow model from bit.ly/1asPx5p.

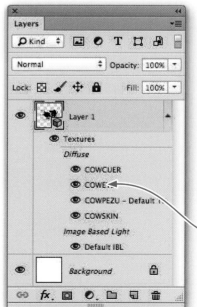

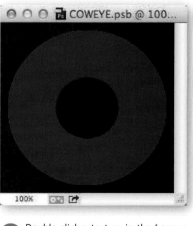

1 There are two ways of viewing placed materials: the first is in the **3D panel**, where they're shown attached to each object. If you want to edit a texture, though, you'll need to find it in the **Layers panel** instead.

2 Double-click a texture in the **Layers panel** to open it in a new **.psb** window. It's interesting to note here that although the eye texture is completely flat, it has a high gloss on the model: this comes from the reflection and shine assigned to the eyeball itself.

3 Most textures are fairly easy to guess. It doesn't take a lot of brain power to work out that *COWSKIN* refers to the main body covering of the cow. When we open it we can see the pattern clearly. We can also see not only the area that represents the udders, but a photograph of an udder that the original artist clearly used for reference.

4 But what are we to make of the texture named *COWCUERN*? Even opening it up in a new window doesn't help much: it's just a rather murky gray texture, in a tiny window, that gives little away.

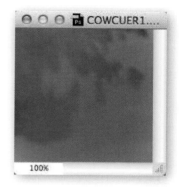

5 There is a fairly straightforward way to work it out. Start by selecting the layer in the **3D panel**, by clicking on it once.

6 As always happens when a single material is selected, the other materials are dimmed out. And as can be seen from the model above, the whole cow has turned pale apart from the horns. It doesn't take much to work out that the texture must apply to those horns.

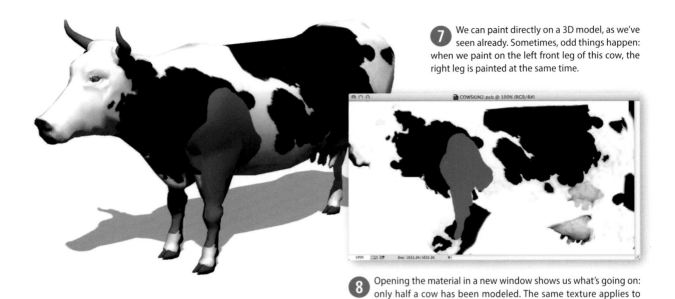

7 We can paint directly on a 3D model, as we've seen already. Sometimes, odd things happen: when we paint on the left front leg of this cow, the right leg is painted at the same time.

8 Opening the material in a new window shows us what's going on: only half a cow has been modeled. The same texture applies to both legs, as well as the other half of the cow.

9 Painting directly on the *Background* layer of the material is never a good idea. Instead, **Undo** any painting operation and make a new layer. **.psb** documents, just like regular Photoshop files, can hold multiple layers.

10 With the material window open, Photoshop makes the painting process easy. As you paint in the new window, the model itself will be painted in real time: there's even a crosshair on the model to show where you're painting.

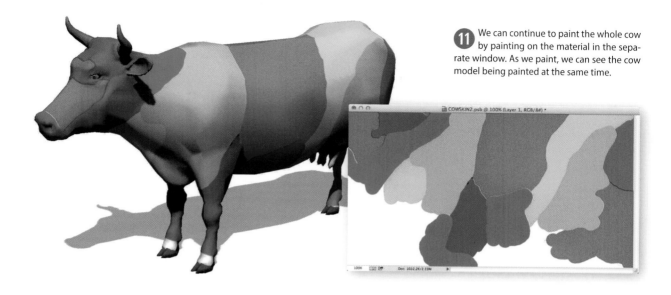

11 We can continue to paint the whole cow by painting on the material in the separate window. As we paint, we can see the cow model being painted at the same time.

12 Because we painted the texture on a new layer, we're able to manipulate it in the same way we'd manipulate any other layer. Here, for instance, we're reducing the opacity to just 50%.

13 Reducing the opacity of the layer instantly makes the layer transparent in the material window. But we won't see the effect immediately on the model: unlike painting, this sort of layer change doesn't take place in real time.

Instead, we need to **Save** the document in order to see the changes made on the 3D model.

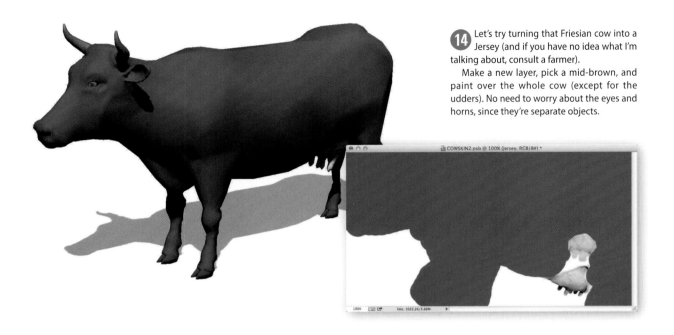

14 Let's try turning that Friesian cow into a Jersey (and if you have no idea what I'm talking about, consult a farmer).

Make a new layer, pick a mid-brown, and paint over the whole cow (except for the udders). No need to worry about the eyes and horns, since they're separate objects.

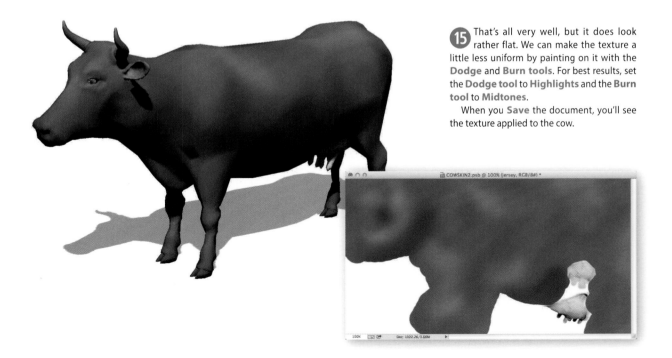

15 That's all very well, but it does look rather flat. We can make the texture a little less uniform by painting on it with the **Dodge** and **Burn tools**. For best results, set the **Dodge tool** to **Highlights** and the **Burn tool** to **Midtones**.

When you **Save** the document, you'll see the texture applied to the cow.

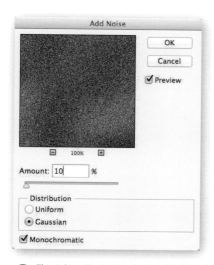

16 To bring a little more life into the texture, first run **Filter > Noise > Add Noise**, with the filter set to **Monochromatic**. A small amount of noise should do the trick: I've used just 10%.

The noise will look a little harsh and artificial – it needs to be softened slightly. So use **Filter > Blur > Gaussian Blur** to smooth out that texture a little way.

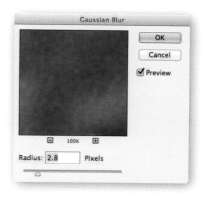

17 This is how the texture looks with the noise and blur applied: it's much more natural in appearance than the flat, plastic look the model had before.

The only remaining step now is to **Save** the material window, so that the changes are made on the model.

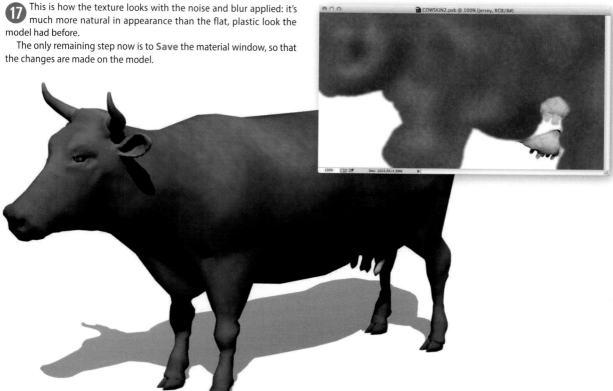

Editing materials in created objects

WHEN YOU ASSIGN A PRESET MATERIAL to a model, you're doing more than just adding a pattern: in most cases you're also adding a bump texture, which determines the apparent height of the surface. Let's see how we can modify and adapt that bump texture to better understand how it works.

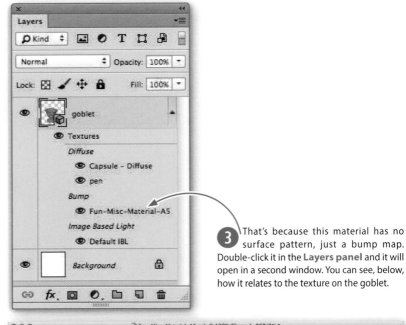

1 This goblet has had the **Fun Textured 1** material applied to it. It wraps around the model, distorting considerably as it's stretched over the thin stem compared to the wide bowl of the goblet.

2 As seen previously, we can double-click the **Diffuse** texture in the **Layers panel** to open it in a new window. But look what happens: it's completely empty.

3 That's because this material has no surface pattern, just a bump map. Double-click it in the **Layers panel** and it will open in a second window. You can see, below, how it relates to the texture on the goblet.

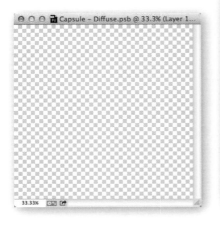

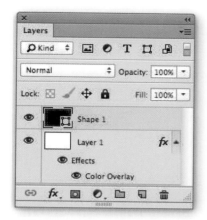

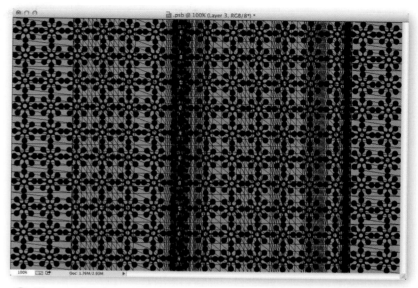

4 When we look at the **Layers panel**, we can see the shape is composed not of a drawn pattern, but of a **Shape** layer placed above a blank layer to which **Layer Effects** have been applied. This is the case with all the built-in textures. The reason is that it makes them all infinitely scalable: unlike drawn patterns, they don't degrade as they're enlarged or stretched over wide surfaces.

5 We can see how the texture is stretched over the surface by choosing **3D > Create Painting Overlay > Wireframes**. This overlays a grid pattern on top of the texture, in a new layer. It can be hard to see what's going on here; if we hide the **Shape** layer, we see just the distortion grid, as seen below.

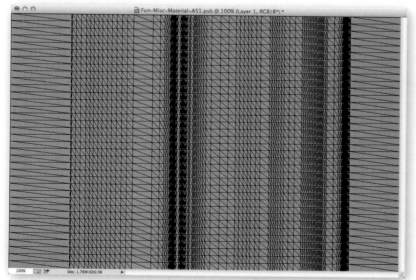

6 The tighter areas, where the lines are densest, are where the texture is most stretched – these are, confusingly, the widest parts of the model. Although it's there for reference only, it will show up on your model if you leave it in place: either delete or hide the layer before rendering.

7 Just for the sake of interest, here's what happens if we **Save** the file with just the wireframe visible: we can see how it wraps around the goblet model.

8 Even with the grid visible, it can be hard to see which parts of the texture belong on which parts of the model. One way to tell is to make a new layer inside the texture file, and simply paint on it.

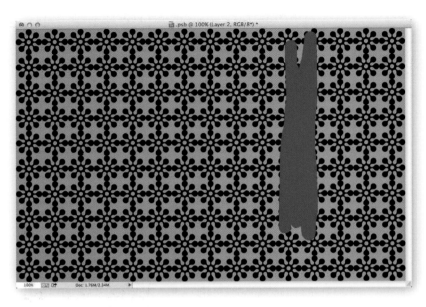

9 Since this is a **bump texture** rather than a regular layer, painting on the texture doesn't add color, but covers up the existing bump map. This produces a smooth, unbumped area on the model.

As we can see here, the area we've painted lines up with the stem of the goblet. That's good: we've identified the area we want to work on. We can now delete the painting layer, as it isn't required any more.

10 Now that we've seen which parts of the pattern align with which areas of the model, let's modify the pattern so we can compensate for the squeezing effect seen on the stem.

Because this is a **Shapes** layer, we can't edit it by painting – we need to modify the paths that construct the layer. Using the **Direct Selection tool** **A**, hold ⌥ *alt* as you drag over half of two columns of the pattern.

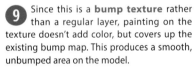

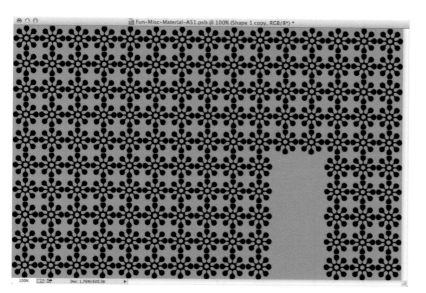

11 Once the paths are selected, just hit **Backspace** to delete them, leaving a hole in the pattern. Now **Save** the texture file.

12 The result: part of the texture has disappeared from the base of the goblet.

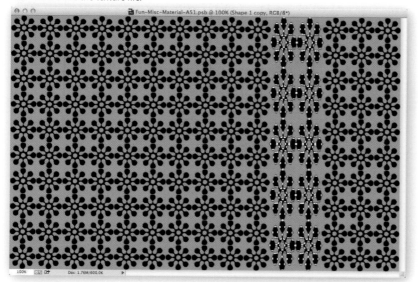

13 To fill that void, select the paths in the upper half of that same column, and use **Free Transform** to scale them so they reach the bottom of the document. In other words, those pattern elements will now individually be twice as high as the originals. As before, **Save** the texture file to continue.

14 Now, with the expanded texture, the stem looks much more in keeping with the remainder of the goblet.

Because the texture is a **Shapes** layer, we can edit it without loss of quality.

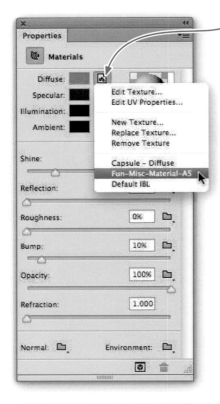

15 With the **bump map** now modified, let's apply it as a pattern as well. From the **Diffuse** pop-up menu at the top of the **Properties panel**, choose the bump map texture by name.

16 It's immediately applied to the goblet – but because it's a grayscale image, all it does is to turn the goblet into two shades of gray. Let's bring some color back into it.

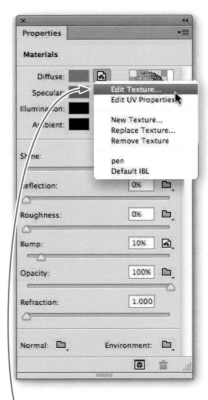

17 Having applied the texture, we can now modify it. Choose **Edit Texture** from the same pop-up menu as before.

18 The texture will once again open in a new window. We can select the **Shapes** layer, pick a new **Foreground Color**, and then simply hit ⌥ Backspace / alt Backspace to fill the shape with that color.

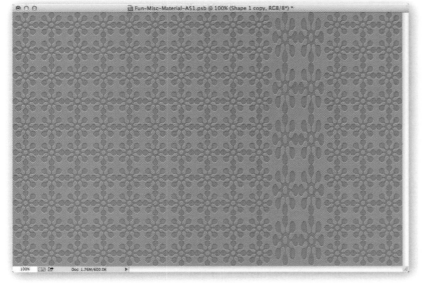

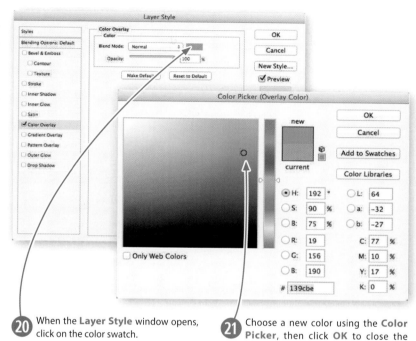

19 The background color is a little more complex, since it's defined as a **Color Overlay** effect. Double-click the item in the **Layers panel** to open the dialog.

20 When the **Layer Style** window opens, click on the color swatch.

21 Choose a new color using the **Color Picker**, then click **OK** to close the picker, and **OK** again to close the dialog.

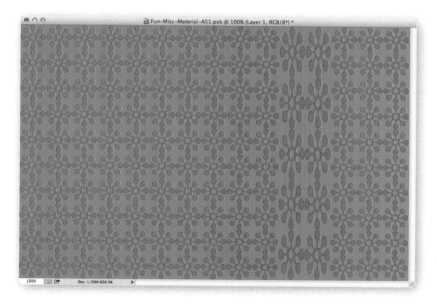

22 When you **Save** the texture file, the new colors will appear on the goblet exactly as expected.

Painting materials from scratch

WE'VE SEEN HOW you can import textures, and how you can modify the built-in presets. But you can also paint complete materials from scratch – not just the color, but the bump map as well. We'll look at some of the basic techniques you can use.

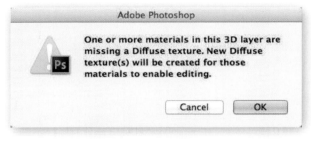

1 We'll use this version of the goblet as the base for our painting. I've tilted it forward so we can see inside it.

2 This object has no textures applied to it. When you first try to paint on it, Photoshop needs to add one: you'll see this dialog. All you have to do is click **OK**.

3 When you agree to a new texture material, you'll be presented with the standard **New** dialog.

You'll have to specify the size you want the texture. Textures for 3D models tend to be small, to reduce file sizes when the models are exported. I've set mine somewhat on the large side at 1000 pixels square, which enables us to see clearly the texture we're working on.

It's most likely that when you create a new texture the **Color Mode** will default to **32 bit**. I recommend changing this to 8 bit before proceeding, to avoid potential problems that might arise later ●

4 When you start to paint, it will feel surprisingly natural – just as if you were painting on a real goblet. Of course, you need to use the **Move tool** to turn it around if you want to paint the other side.

5 When you paint across a gap, from one part of the object to another, Photoshop will do its best to paint where it thinks you intend. Notice how a spot of blue appears at the top, on the far side of the object.

6 That's because the texture is automatically mirrored, so it wraps around both sides of the goblet at the same time. The green paint on the base, for instance, is mirrored as you paint.

7 You can use any of the painting tools directly on your object, not just the standard brush. Here, I've used the **Smudge tool** to smear the paint so that it appears to be more naturally painted onto the surface.

8 Bear in mind that, at all times, you're painting on a three-dimensional surface. Here, I've painted a vertical orange line right down the center of the goblet.

9 When the object is rotated about its vertical axis, you can see how the orange line is in fact curved over the extrusion surface of the goblet. It's also thinner over thinner areas, such as the stem.

3D painting methods

THERE ARE TWO SEPARATE methods for painting onto 3D surfaces: Projection and Texture. Of the two, Texture is the one you'll use most often. But if you created a new Diffuse texture in 32-bit mode, as seen on the previous pages, you'd be limited to using only the Projection method.

1 The **Projection** method behaves as if the paint is shone onto the surface like a light. As far as possible, it treats the surface as if it wasn't there.

2 The second method is **Texture**, which wraps around the surface in a more organic way. This is the most usual system, and it's the one we'll be using throughout this chapter.

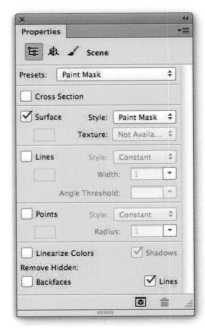

3 You'll notice that it's tricky to paint around the edges of objects. If you choose the **Paint Mask** preset from the **Scene** pane in the **Properties panel**, you'll see the hard-to-paint areas in red.

4 You can also use **3D > Select Paintable Areas** to select just those regions that can be painted on. You can see here how that selection aligns exactly with the red areas shown in the previous step.

Painting bump textures

WE'VE SEEN HOW BUMP TEXTURES can be used to simulate surface lumpiness. But as well as importing bump maps and generating them from the Diffuse texture, we can also paint them directly onto our 3D objects, using a variety of methods.

2 When you now paint on the surface in black, it will appear to be slightly recessed.

If you want to make the surface appear higher rather than lower, first fill the bump map with gray and then paint on the model in white.

1 To begin, use **3D > Paint on Target Texture > Bump**. You'll see the same dialog as we saw before, and will be asked to specify a new texture size.

3 You can get interesting results by changing the mode of the brush. Here, we've chosen **Dissolve** mode, which produces a spray of tiny dots.

4 The effect is to produce a strong roughening effect on the surface wherever you paint. To paint with fewer dots, reduce the **opacity** of the brush.

5 If you paint over the same area several times, you'll find the roughness disappearing. This isn't a bug: it's just that you've filled that area with solid black, rather than leaving the individual dots visible.

Painting transparency

AS WELL AS COLORS and surface texture, materials can contain transparency – we've seen this already in the preset material Fun Textured 3. Adding transparency gives an extra dimension to 3D modeling, and allows for the creation of much more complex forms.

1 Use **3D > Paint on Target Texture > Opacity**. You'll see the same dialog as we saw before, and will be asked to specify a new texture size.

While you're painting in black, you'll see partial transparency – but it's more as if you're painting on the surface with a dark gray.

2 When you release the mouse button, you can see how the painting has made the object truly transparent.

It's interesting to note that only the front surface – the one you're painting on – becomes transparent: the inner surface of this goblet remains resolutely opaque.

3 Even having painted the outer skin away, we still can't paint transparency on that inner surface – at least, not from this side. Instead, we need to paint it from the other side, by painting inside the goblet.

4 For more control, double-click the **Opacity** layer in the **Layers panel** and it will open in a new window (left). You can paint on here, or create rectangular areas filled with black, to hide the model; you have to **Save** the document to see the effect.

When working in this way, get into the habit of creating a new layer for each new element you want to add. That way, you'll be able to move the objects around more easily, saving after each move so you can see how they affect the model.

5 Rotating the texture will, of course, rotate the way in which the transparency is applied. But the result isn't always predictable: complex surfaces can take transparency in surprising ways.

6 Sometimes we need to fiddle with a transparency layer to get it right. The round dots here have come out as ellipses.

7 By distorting the dots in the opacity map, we're able to produce round dots on the object itself.

8 You're not limited to just painting and regular-shaped blocks of color, of course. Here, I've used an intricate pattern taken from a piece of wallpaper to create this spectacular fruit bowl.

Painting on material windows

PAINTING DIRECTLY ONTO OBJECTS is all very well, but it's a little lacking in control. For precise painting work, you're better off painting onto the diffuse material window instead.

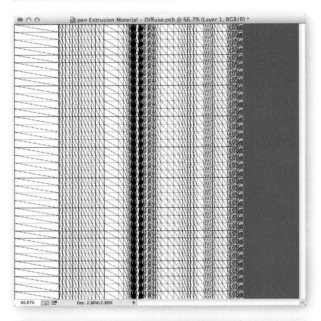

1 Make a new **Diffuse** texture, and open its window; then choose **3D > Create Painting Overlay > Wireframe** so you can see where you're painting. This helps to align the texture with the model.

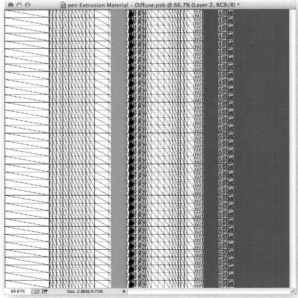

2 Because we can see the wireframe both in the texture window and on the model, we're able to identify painting locations with more ease than the hit-and-miss approach would allow.

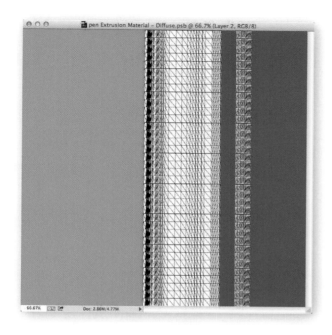

3 To fill large areas, such as the interior of the goblet, it's easier to make a selection with the **Marquee tool** and then fill that with color. You'll then need to **Save** to see the results on the model.

4 Even though the aim is to completely fill the model with color, it still makes sense to paint on a separate layer from the Wireframe overlay. Use new layers whenever you can to allow for easier later editing.

5 You're not limited to just painting, of course. Any object can be brought in and placed as part of the texture – or you can create your own intricate patterns from scratch for more variety.

6 When the painting is finished, you can give the object extra presence by making it into a **bump texture** as well. In the **Properties panel**, with the **Texture** pane visible, choose the texture from the pop-up menu next to the Bump item.

Painting on complex surfaces

PHOTOSHOP ALLOWS YOU to paint directly onto 3D models, wrapping the paint around the surface of the object as you use the brush, smudge tool, or any of the painting tools. There are some special considerations, though, that affect how the paint works on the surface.

1 The default painting method is **Texture**, which produces the smoothest results. When you paint on just one part of the model, you're able to use this method to paint in fine detail.

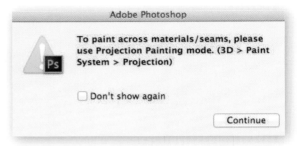

2 When you try to paint on multiple surfaces, though, you'll see this warning message. As instructed, use **3D > Paint System > Projection** to switch to the other painting method.

3 Now, you can paint across several surfaces – the body, the door, the chrome trim. But the effect is more ragged, and it's harder to produce smooth edges this way.

4 The default painting method is on the **Diffuse** material – in other words, painting with color. But you can paint on other materials: use **3D > Paint on Target Texture >** to select the material type. You'll be prompted to create a new material for each surface you paint on.

5 Here, I've painted on the front of this car on the **Bump** material, which gives it this beaten-up look. The ability to paint this effect directly onto the car body gives us tremendous control over the look.

6 You can vary the brush type to achieve different results. Here, I've also painted on the **Bump** texture, but I've set the brush to paint in **Dissolve** mode, at low opacity, producing this dimpled look.

7 Sometimes you find you want to paint on an area that can't be easily seen, such as the seats inside this car. It's easy to paint the visible portions, but those beneath the car door are hidden from view.

8 The solution here is to make a selection of the area you want to hide. You can use the **Lasso tool**, the **Marquee tool**, or any of the painting tools to make the initial selection.

9 Once you 've made the selection, choose **3D > Show/Hide Polygons > Hide Selection**, or use the shortcut ⌘ ⌥ X ctrl alt X. This removes the front surface of the selection.

10 That's all very well, but that view left us seeing the inside of the door. No problem: repeat the shortcut, or use the menu option again, to hide further layers of the car.

11 With the door hidden, you can now paint the seats in full. Use **3D > Show/Hide Polygons > Invert Selection** to show just the hidden areas, and **Show All** to reveal the car in its entirety.

12 For more accurate painting, select **Scene** in the **3D panel**, then in the **Properties panel**, from the **Style** pop-up menu, choose **Unlit Texture** to show the car with no shading.

Other painting modes

AS WELL AS PAINTING diffuse textures, bump maps and opacity, we're able to paint a range of other characteristics in and out of our models. Here's a selection of the available options. All the painting modes are chosen using 3D > Paint on Target Texture.

Specular: This mode only affects the highlights. The top highlight has been painted pink; the lower one, on the base, remains in its original color.

Shininess: Where the model has been painted it's brighter – but it's less shiny in that there's now a smaller distinction between the bright and dark areas.

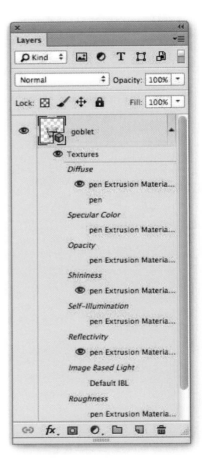

Reflectivity: This affects how an object reflects its surroundings. We haven't looked at reflections yet – we'll do so in the next section of this book.

Self-illumination: This mode starts with a completely invisible object, which becomes visible where it's painted. Best for objects that have been turned into light sources.

All the different material types are shown in the **Layers panel**, listed beneath one another. You can choose which ones you want to view, and they can all be disabled by turning them off one at a time – click the **eye** icon next to the name of each texture.

PART THREE

Building
3D scenes

PART THREE
Building
3D scenes

12 Multiple objects

WE'VE LOOKED CLOSELY at building, lighting and texturing 3D objects so far in this book. But we've only looked at working with individual models. And that's all very well – you can go a long way with modeling, lighting and rendering just one object at a time.

But things really start getting interesting when you combine several objects into a single scene. Take the simple example below: the dog is a 3D model downloaded from archive3d.com; the hoop has been created directly in Photoshop by extruding a circular path, revolving it 360° and then expanding the extrusion depth. The trouble is, how do we make the dog jump through the hoop? As two separate objects they can't interact, even though they're in the same document, because they're on two different layers.

The solution is to merge them together so they're both part of the same layer – and therefore both part of the same 3D scene. Now, we can interact the two models and the dog jumps through the hoop.

Creating and combining

TO EXPLAIN THE PROCESS we'll begin with the wine bottle we worked with on page 56, then make a simple hoop and combine the two in a single layer. This will also give us the opportunity to look at object alignment, which becomes critical when working with multiple models.

1 We made this bottle from a primitive object earlier in the book. I've darkened the glass and made the foil cap red.

Open this model, which you'll find on the **3DPhotoshop. net** website.

2 Make a new layer, then use the **Shapes tool** set to create **paths**, and draw a circle. Use the **3D panel** to extrude that path, and you'll see a small, squat cylinder like the one above right.

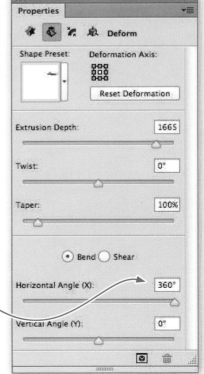

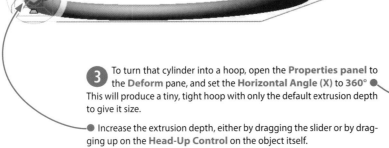

3 To turn that cylinder into a hoop, open the **Properties panel** to the **Deform** pane, and set the **Horizontal Angle (X)** to **360°** This will produce a tiny, tight hoop with only the default extrusion depth to give it size.

● Increase the extrusion depth, either by dragging the slider or by dragging up on the **Head-Up Control** on the object itself.

4 We can bring the hoop down over the bottle, even setting its orientation to match the angle of the bottle.

But the one thing we can't do is poke the bottle through the hoop. The hoop's layer is in front of the bottle layer, so – just as with any pair of Photoshop layers – the hoop is wholly in front of the bottle.

We can, of course, drag the hoop layer *behind* the bottle layer, as I've done on the right. But now, as you'd expect, the hoop is entirely behind the bottle.

5 When we look at the **Layers panel**, we can see that the hoop and the bottle are two entirely separate layers, and that's why we can't get them to interact (well, we could, but only by making a Layer Mask for one or the other of them).

6 The solution is to select both the bottle and hoop layers in the **Layers panel**, and merge them together either by choosing **Layer > Merge Layers** or by using the keyboard shortcut ⌘ E ctrl E.

As you can see, the two layers have now merged into a single layer, and as standard that layer will take on the name of the lower layer in the selection – in this case, it's *bottle* ●

It looks as if the two objects have become just one object. But what we're actually seeing is a single 3D scene, rather than a single object.

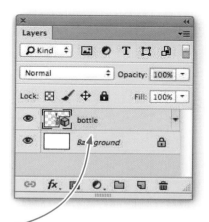

7 When we look at the **3D panel**, we can see the bottle and the hoop clearly listed as two separate objects. As part of a single 3D scene, they even cast shadows on one another.

Note that the position of the merged objects will change relative to one another when two 3D layers are merged, often dramatically so. That's because they started with different ground plane orientations, and when the layers are merged it's these ground planes that are aligned.

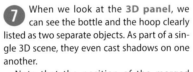

8 We can select either the hoop or the bottle by clicking on it with the **Move tool**, or by selecting it in the **3D panel**. We can now either use the **3D Axis** or just drag on the edges of the bounding box to rotate the hoop around the bottle.

9 It all looks fine – there's the hoop still visible behind the bottle. But when we check out the **Secondary View**, we can see the problem: the hoop is actually passing *through* the bottle, rather than behind it.

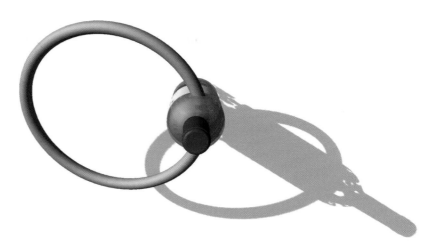

10 To check what's going on, we can spin the whole view around, making sure no objects are selected first. When we look from above in the main view, we can clearly see the hoop going through the bottle.

When we're working normally in Photoshop, this sort of thing doesn't matter: if it looks right, then it is right. But with 3D scenes we might want to turn the whole scene around to view it from a different angle – and that's where problems will start to arise. It's worth taking the time to get it right in the first instance, to avoid potential problems further down the line.

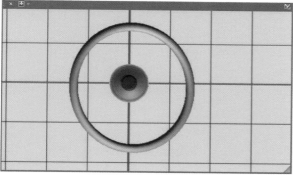

11 The intersection issue is actually a very easy problem to fix: all we have to do is to move the hoop, using the **Secondary View** for reference, until it's centered on the bottle. This view is much more important when working with more than one object in a scene.

12 Here's the scene with the intersection problem corrected. It may not look much different to how it appeared in step 8, but the two objects will now behave much more like items in the real world when it comes to refraction, transparency and shadow-casting.

Manipulating objects in a scene

1 As we've seen, when two 3D objects are merged into a single layer, both objects now appear as separate items in the **3D panel**.

You can manipulate the view of the whole scene by dragging it with the **Move tool** when no objects are selected. If you want to work on an individual object, there are two ways to select it: either click on the object itself, or click on its folder in the **3D panel**.

A selected object is indicated by the bounding box, as well as being highlighted in the panel.

2 You can pop open an object's folder to see its contents. This will show the materials used and, if the object is composed of several parts, as this wine bottle is, it will also show all the parts listed as separate **meshes** within the folder.

To manipulate the entire object, make sure the folder itself is selected, rather than just one of its constituent parts.

3 As well as selecting the whole object, you can select just a single item within the assembly and manipulate just that on its own. Here, the label mesh has been slid out to one side.

Note how the label is also interacting with the hoop, which now passes through it. All objects within a single scene will interact with each other in exactly the same way.

When you download or otherwise import models, you may well find that they aren't already neatly sorted into folders. In this case, you'll often find that when you attempt to move a whole object, you only move one of its parts. Be sure the whole thing is selected first – or place all the parts into a new folder yourself.

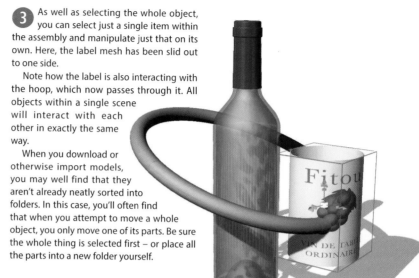

4 A single item within an object group can interact with other objects within that group, as well as with other objects in the same scene.

Here, the bottle cap has been selected, and slid vertically downward. You can see how it has penetrated inside the bottle neck, whose transparency allows it to be clearly visible inside it.

Duplicating objects

1 As well as importing objects from a variety of sources, we can duplicate objects within a 3D scene. To do this, select the object in the **3D panel** and click on the pop-up menu in the top right: choose **Duplicate Object**.

2 When you duplicate an object, the scene won't look any different. That's because it will be duplicated directly on top of the original.

If you look at the **3D panel**, though, you'll see the duplicate clearly listed below the original.

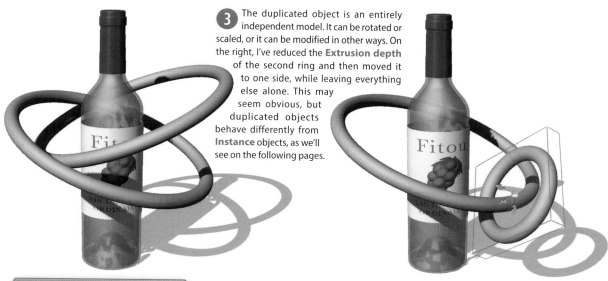

3 The duplicated object is an entirely independent model. It can be rotated or scaled, or it can be modified in other ways. On the right, I've reduced the **Extrusion depth** of the second ring and then moved it to one side, while leaving everything else alone. This may seem obvious, but duplicated objects behave differently from **Instance** objects, as we'll see on the following pages.

4 Objects can also be deleted from a 3D scene, again using the pop-up menu in the corner of the **3D panel**. Choose **Delete Objects** from the pop-up menu list.

Move Object to Ground Plane

Select Paintable Areas
Create Painting Overlay ▶

Add Lights Preset...
Replace Lights Presets...
Save Lights Preset...
Delete Current Lights Preset

Add Objects ▶
Delete Objects
Duplicate Object
Instance Object
Bake Object
Ungroup Objects
Reverse Order

Render

Export 3D Layer...

Close
Close Tab Group

Photoshop CS6 users

If you're using Photoshop CS6, then the tools listed on this page won't apply, as they hadn't been introduced yet. There's no simple way to duplicate or delete objects via a menu option.

You can still merge objects together in a single scene, but if you want more than one, here's the workaround:

● First, duplicate the **3D layer** containing the object of which you want multiple copies, once for each copy.

● Select all the layers, and merge them together.

There's no way to delete an object from a 3D scene in Photoshop CS6. The best you can do is to make it as small as you can and hide it inside another object.

Instancing objects

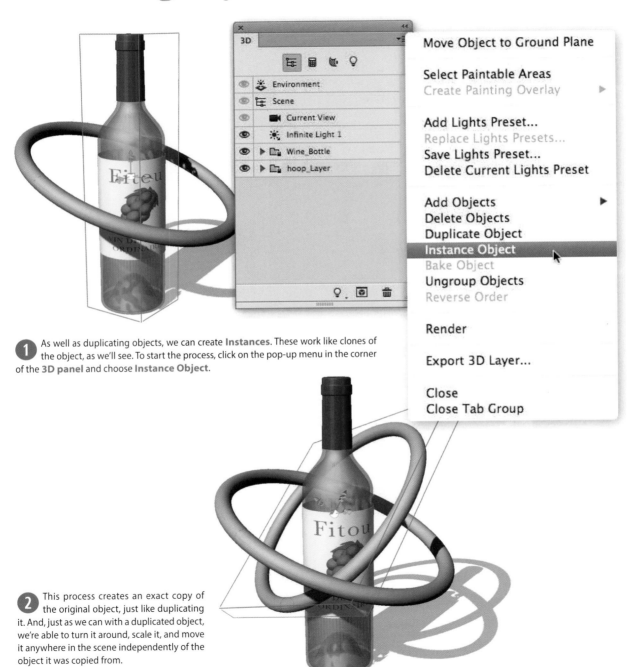

1 As well as duplicating objects, we can create **Instances**. These work like clones of the object, as we'll see. To start the process, click on the pop-up menu in the corner of the **3D panel** and choose **Instance Object**.

2 This process creates an exact copy of the original object, just like duplicating it. And, just as we can with a duplicated object, we're able to turn it around, scale it, and move it anywhere in the scene independently of the object it was copied from.

3 The difference comes when we manipulate the construction of the object, rather than simply rotating and moving it.

On the left, I've reduced the **Extrusion Depth** of the instanced hoop. As you can see, this action has reduced the extrusion of both hoops, making them both smaller.

4 When we paint onto an instanced object, the paint appears on both instances simultaneously – it doesn't matter which one we paint on, as they're seen as exact replicas of each other.

5 The same goes for applying any of the built-in materials to an instanced object: the same material will be applied to both at the same time.

We can even edit the **Source** of the object – in this example, it's the path that defined the original circle on which the hoop is based – and when we do so, both objects change to reflect the new shape of the path.

Photoshop CS6 users

There is no equivalent of Instances in Photoshop CS6. In order to reproduce the effect, you'd have to perform the same adjustments to each object individually.

De-instancing objects

1 Any **Instance** of an object can be made into a regular, detached object by a process rather bizarrely named **baking**.

If you select an object group in the **3D panel** and go to the pop-up menu, though, you'll find that the item **Bake Object** is grayed out.

2 Rather than selecting the **Group**, you have to pop it open and select the individual **Mesh** within that group.

Now, you'll find the **Bake Object** menu item can be selected from the menu.

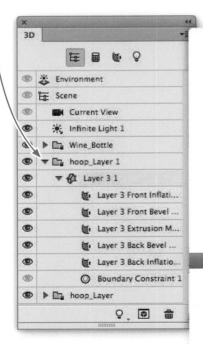

3 Once it's baked, the instanced object can now be treated independently.

13 Refraction, reflection and transparency

WHEN WE COMBINE 3D models, we need to be concerned with how they interact with each other on a physical level – making sure they only intersect if we want them to, preventing them from crashing into one another, ensuring they're all sitting flat on the Ground Plane so they cast appropriate shadows.

But if we've used transparent or reflective materials, we need to consider how the models behave when seen through each other. How much does a bowl refract the view seen through it? How much reflection should there be on a flat surface? How fast should that reflection fade away? Just how opaque is a glass bottle?

Photoshop can handle many different kinds of material, with a large degree of control over how the materials interact with one another. In this chapter, we'll look at how to tell Photoshop to construct the scene exactly according to our perception of the world.

Creating transparency

TO MAKE THIS SCENE we'll combine two objects: a photograph of an apple, inflated using the technique described on page 46, and a version of the goblet we modeled on page 30, which I've reshaped to make it more of a fruit bowl.

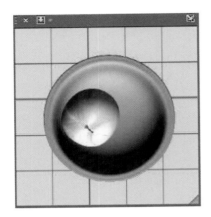

1 The first step is to merge the two layers together, so that they're both part of the same 3D scene. When positioning the apple within the bowl, it greatly helps to have the **Secondary View** open, so you can see exactly how the two objects fit together.

2 It's easy to duplicate the apple within the 3D scene, using the pop-up menu in the **3D panel**. Positioning them both is a little trickier; the **Secondary View** certainly helps, but it's hard to avoid the objects crashing into each other. As I've said before, Photoshop doesn't include any collision detection.

I've rotated the duplicated apple, both spinning it about its vertical axis and turning it so it's tilted away from us. This helps to obscure the fact that it's a precise copy of the original apple.

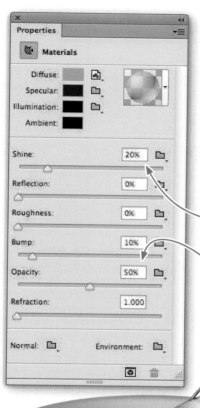

3 Click twice on the bowl with the **Move tool** to open the **Materials** pane in the **Properties panel**.

Click the swatch next to the **Diffuse** item in the panel, and choose a bottle green to tint the bowl.

Because it's going to be made of glass, we need to make a couple more changes:

● Raise the **Shine** amount to make it glossy.

● Drop the **Opacity** so we can see the apples through it.

There are many other changes we can make later, but for now let's see what difference those make.

4 Here's the bowl as it now appears. The tint has changed the color, and we can see the apples through it. But it's very hard to tell what's going on: Photoshop will display transparency in this mottled way in Preview mode.

5 We have to **Render** the scene to see it smoothly. And we can see the first problem: the shape of the original path is clearly visible.

6 We can get rid of that path by selecting the **Front** and **Back Inflation** materials, and setting their **Opacity** to zero.

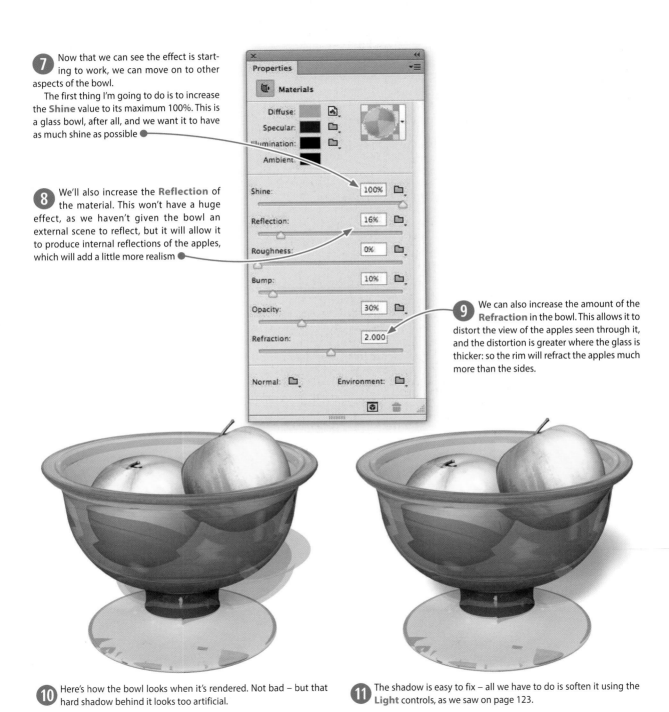

7 Now that we can see the effect is starting to work, we can move on to other aspects of the bowl.

The first thing I'm going to do is to increase the **Shine** value to its maximum 100%. This is a glass bowl, after all, and we want it to have as much shine as possible ●

8 We'll also increase the **Reflection** of the material. This won't have a huge effect, as we haven't given the bowl an external scene to reflect, but it will allow it to produce internal reflections of the apples, which will add a little more realism ●

9 We can also increase the amount of the **Refraction** in the bowl. This allows it to distort the view of the apples seen through it, and the distortion is greater where the glass is thicker: so the rim will refract the apples much more than the sides.

10 Here's how the bowl looks when it's rendered. Not bad – but that hard shadow behind it looks too artificial.

11 The shadow is easy to fix – all we have to do is soften it using the **Light** controls, as we saw on page 123.

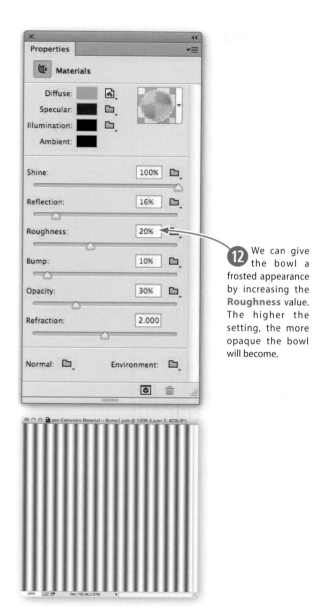

12 We can give the bowl a frosted appearance by increasing the **Roughness** value. The higher the setting, the more opaque the bowl will become.

13 As with all these settings, you really don't get much idea of how it's going to look until you **Render** the scene. But remember that you can render just a part of it for a quick impression.

14 We can add further texture to the bowl by adding a **Bump texture**. First, click the folder icon next to the **Bump** item in the **Properties panel**, then choose *New Texture*. Pick a size – around 500 pixels is enough – and click OK. Nothing will happen; you must then choose *Edit Texture* from the same menu. I've added a series of black lines, which I've then blurred using **Filter > Blur > Gaussian Blur**.

15 This is how the bowl looks with the **Bump** texture applied. The texture is rotated 90°, and produces this striped appearance.

Refraction by shape and number

THE AMOUNT TO WHICH an object refracts those around it depends on the Refractive Index of the material, which is set in the Properties panel. But it also depends to a greater extent on the *shape* of the object doing the refracting: a thick object will refract much more than a thin one, simply because there's so much more material to bend the view seen through it.

But a thick flat object will barely show the refraction. It's the variation in the object's surface shape that produces the distinctive distortion we associate with looking through glass.

1 This glass ball has a Refraction setting of **1.000** – which means it doesn't refract the background at all. You can see it's there, because it has an **Opacity** of **20%**, but it doesn't look anything like glass.

2 Increasing the Refraction to just **1.100** produces this huge amount of distortion. That's because of the shape: as a sphere, it has an extreme range of thickness between the outside and the center.

3 Increasing the refraction to a middle value of **1.500** turns the view completely on its head.

4 Here, I've duplicated the original text and moved it forward. I then made it thinner, with a smaller extrusion amount, and set its **Opacity** to **20%**.

But with the Refraction set to 1.000, it doesn't look anything like glass.

5 When the Refraction is increased to **1.200**, the object takes on a much glassier look. But that's more because of the refraction at the *edges*, rather than that seen through the face of the lettering.

6 Tilting the second set of lettering exaggerates the refraction, making it look even more like a real transparent object.

The tilt produces an increased amount of refraction, because we're now looking at the object through a thicker angle of glass.

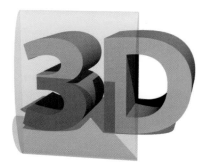

7 This is a traditional curved lens shape with a flat back, placed in front of the lettering. I've left the Refraction at **1.000** here to show the shape.

8 With the Refraction set to just **1.200**, you'd expect to see little distortion. But at the top, where the angle of incidence is stronger, there's more distortion.

9 With a Refraction amount of **1.400**, there's now significantly more refraction in the middle of the lens.

10 With the Refraction raised to **1.600**, the text is stretched even higher – but there's little apparent difference between this and the previous setting.

11 When the Refraction is set at **2.000**, the distortion becomes extreme. We're also starting to see some internal reflections as the light is bounced around the inside.

12 At the maximum setting of **3.000**, we can now see almost nothing except those internal reflections.

13 Refraction on its own can be enough to indicate the presence of a glassy material. The horizontal cylinder in this image has an **Opacity** setting of **0%**, which means it's effectively invisible. Only the refraction of the text behind it gives a clue as to its presence in the scene.

Reflections on the ground

IF AN OBJECT is standing on a reflective surface, such as marble or metal, or even on a wet surface, we'd expect to be able to see some reflection in that surface. Photoshop has simple built-in tools for creating those reflections, and for modifying their appearance.

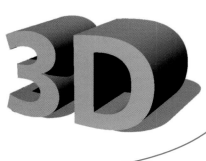

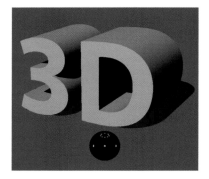

1 This is the 3D model we created in Chapter 1. Begin by choosing the **Environment** item, right at the top of the **3D panel**.

2 When you select it, you'll see the **Image-Based Light** overlaid on top – the default is mainly gray. Switch to the **Marquee tool M** to hide this overlay.

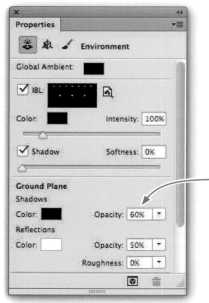

3 The **Properties panel** will now display the **Environment** settings in full. The region that interests us is the **Reflections** setting at the bottom.
To add a reflection, drag left or right on the word **Opacity**, or type an opacity value into the number field

4 You'll see the reflection appearing immediately on your object. Now is a good time to make sure it's sitting flat on the **Ground Plane**, or the reflection will be detached from it.

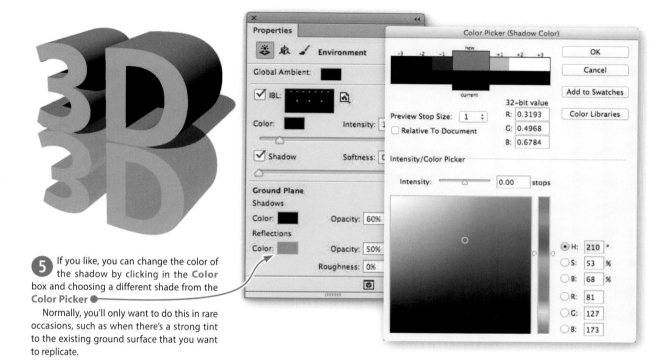

5 If you like, you can change the color of the shadow by clicking in the **Color** box and choosing a different shade from the **Color Picker**.

Normally, you'll only want to do this in rare occasions, such as when there's a strong tint to the existing ground surface that you want to replicate.

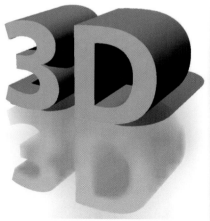

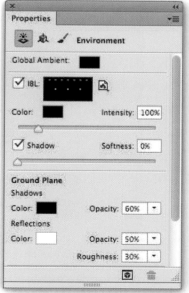

6 The **Roughness** setting determines the manner in which the reflection fades away. With the roughness set to **30%**, the preview shows a very approximate impression of what it will look like.

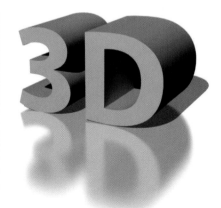

7 You need to **Render** the scene in order to see the reflection as it will finally appear. You can see here the difference between this rendered view and the preview we saw in the previous step.

Reflection between objects

AS WELL AS REFLECTING objects in the Ground Plane, we can of course reflect them in each other. Materials such as Gold and Steel, which always look disappointingly dull when they're first applied, take on much more of a luster when they have something to reflect.

1 This is the fruit bowl we used on page 184, in which we made the bowl out of frosted glass. I've redrawn the outline to make it a flatter bowl, so we can see how the inside reflects the apples.

2 I've made a few changes to the **Materials** pane of the **Properties panel**. I've changed the color from green to a dark gray, and raised the **Opacity** to 100%; I've also increased the **Reflection** amount to 50%, using the settings below. You can see a faint reflection.

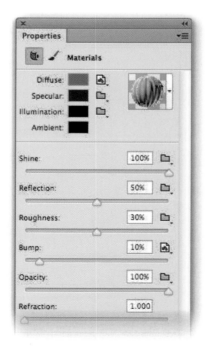

3 The ripples in the base of the bowl aren't part of the real shape of the model, but are generated by the **Bump texture** we applied earlier. You can disable this by clicking on the icon next to the **Bump** item in the panel, and choosing **Edit Texture** from the pop-up menu.

When the texture opens in a new window, there's no need to delete the fuzzy lines that create the effect: hide the layer by clicking the eye icon next to it in the **Layers panel**, then save the texture.

The preview above shows the bump map hidden – but you won't see the reflection in preview mode.

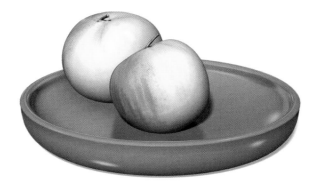

4 When you now **Render** the scene, you'll see the reflection of the apples showing up inside the flattened bowl. It's still very low key, though, for a couple of reasons.

5 The first issue is that we'd applied a **Roughness** setting of 30% to this bowl, when it was masquerading as glass. Now that it's shiny metal, we can remove that roughness altogether.

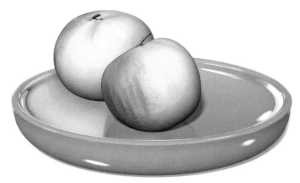

6 Increasing the **Reflection** amount to 100% produces much stronger reflections. You can see how the reflection of the apples is distorted by the curved interior of the bowl.

7 Let's try bringing that **bump map** back, by revealing its texture layer – reversing the process in step 3. Without the **Roughness** and with the higher **Reflection**, it creates interesting reflections.

8 Of course, we're not stuck with choosing between reflection and transparency. Here, I've mixed together a whole load of effects: the bowl has been given a degree of transparency back, and I've added a soft shadow beneath it.

What's interesting here is how Photoshop calculates the complex ray tracing involved. The apples are refracted through the transparent bowl onto the ground reflection – there's really an awful lot going on here.

Image-Based Lighting

IMAGE-BASED LIGHTING, often abbreviated to IBL, is a texture that produces reflections over an entire scene – it is, in effect, the environment that the objects reflect.

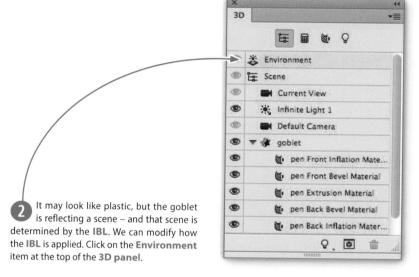

1 This is a modified version of the goblet we introduced much earlier in this book. I've applied a basic gold texture to it, but as you can see it looks more like plastic than real gold.

2 It may look like plastic, but the goblet is reflecting a scene – and that scene is determined by the **IBL**. We can modify how the **IBL** is applied. Click on the **Environment** item at the top of the **3D panel**.

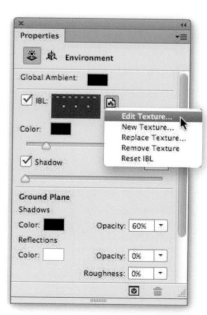

3 When the panel opens, you'll see a dark gray overlay over the image. In the middle is a ball, on which the **IBL** has been mapped. In fact, that's a representation of the sphere that's *outside* the whole scene.

4 Drag around in this window to rotate the sphere, and you'll see how the shine pattern moves around the object.

The thumbnail in the **Properties panel** shows the **IBL** in miniature. Click on the icon to the right, and select **Edit Texture**.

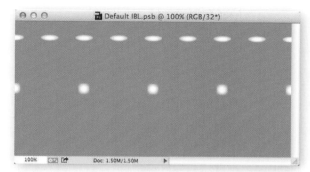

5 The **IBL** will open in a new window. The default image is made of a flat gray field on which are two rows of different-sized dots: these represent photographic lighting. You can also display them more prominently by dragging them.

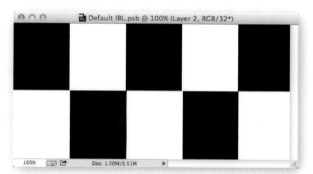

6 **IBL** images that work best are those with low contrast. This checkerboard is much too highly contrasted, producing an over-bright scene. White should be used as an occasional highlight.

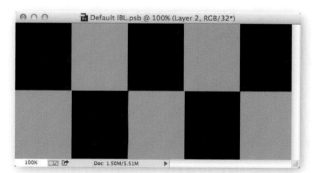

7 Reducing the brightness of the checkerboard creates a much more subtle lighting effect. You can also use photographic scenes as Image-Based Lights. We'll be looking at this in the next chapter.

Painting Image-Based Lights

YOU CAN PAINT DIRECTLY onto an IBL texture, and the effects will be seen on the object as you paint – just as it is when you paint on a texture. The object is likely to be affected in unpredictable ways, though, so always work on a new layer and be prepared to Undo a lot if it doesn't look right.

1 Here's the original, default IBL texture applied to the goblet. It looks very dull.

2 Make a new layer, and paint dark streaks on it. You'll see the changes in real time, as you paint.

3 You can also paint color directly onto the IBL texture, to give the impression of it reflecting a colored object.

4 Painting highlights can produce a dramatic effect, but needs to be used sparingly.

14 Combining models with photographs

CREATING 3D MODELS in isolation is an essential part of the modeling process, as are adding texture and lighting. But models don't need to exist just one at a time, or even just in conjunction with other 3D models. Images can be so much more expressive and lifelike when models are combined with photographs – and we are working in Photoshop, after all.

When you add photographs, though, several more considerations come into play. What happens about transparency? How is the view reflected and refracted by glass elements? Does the surface reflect the objects? What direction is the lighting coming from? Making 3D elements look like they belong in a scene is the most taxing part of 3D modeling, but it can also be the most rewarding.

Interaction: moving the model back

THE EASIEST WAY to combine a photograph with a 3D object is simply to place them both in the same scene. We'll start by building a hollow box, and then we'll move it so the man is sitting on it.

1 You'll find the Photoshop file with this man on **3DPhotoshop.net**, so you can try it out for yourself.

2 The box is simply a square frame, extruded to make a new 3D object and filled with a wood texture.

3 Scale the box down, and rotate it a little. Scaling works from the center, which is why it's now too high in the scene.

4 Use the **Properties panel** to select the **Mesh** view, then press **Move to Ground** to resite the object.

5 You'll probably need to move the **Ground Plane** to position the box correctly, so click away from the object to deselect it. It will help to start with the **Drag tool**, as seen above, to move the scene down; then switch back to the **Rotate tool** to position it more closely.

6 To move the cube behind the man, all you have to do is drag the 3D layer beneath the man layer in the **Layers panel**. You'll probably then find you need to rotate and move the cube around a little more – but move it by dragging on the vertical faces, so you don't lift it off the Ground Plane.

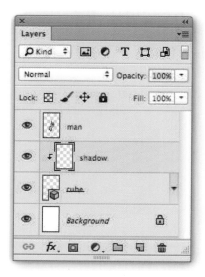

7 The final step is to create a shadow for the man. Make a new layer, and use **Layer > Create Clipping Mask** so it's only visible where it overlaps the layer beneath.

With the foreground color set to black, use a soft-edged brush at a low opacity (about 30%) to paint in shadows beneath the man's legs.

Because the layer uses the cube as a Clipping Mask, the shadow will only appear over the cube layer.

Interaction with Layer Masks

AS THE NEXT STEP in the process of combining images with 3D models, we'll place the man inside the box we've already created. The easiest way to do this is simply to make a Layer Mask.

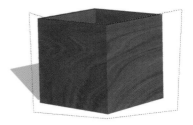

1 Rotate the box so that the open side is pointing upward – previously, it was pointing forward.

2 Enlarge the box slightly, drop it back onto the Ground Plane, and move it so the man is sitting on the rear side.

3 Hide the man layer, then use the **Lasso tool** to select the front two sides. Hold ⌥ *alt* to trace straight lines.

4 Reveal the man layer once again, and choose **Layer > Layer Mask > Hide Selection**. This places the legs in the box.

5 You may well find a piece of the man sticking out, such as his right toe. Paint over it in black on the Layer Mask to hide it.

6 Make a new layer, using the man as a **Clipping Mask**, to paint a shadow over his legs.

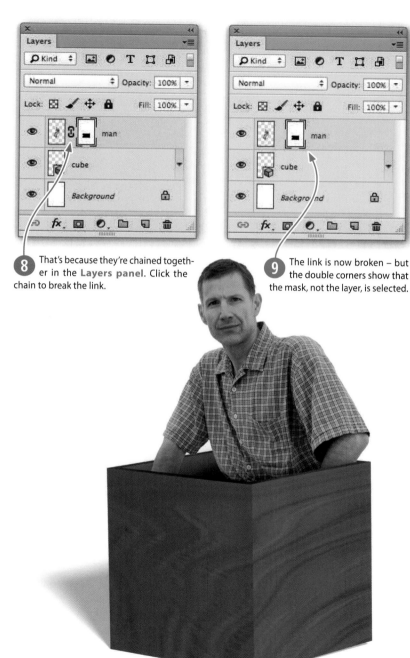

7 When we try to move the man down, we find that the Layer Mask moves down with him.

8 That's because they're chained together in the **Layers panel**. Click the chain to break the link.

9 The link is now broken – but the double corners show that the mask, not the layer, is selected.

10 Make sure the layer is selected, and not the mask – click on it in the **Layers panel** to ensure it has double corners, indicating that it is selected.

Now, the man can be moved independently of the mask.

Interaction with cross sections

THERE ARE TIMES when simply adding a Layer Mask to an image isn't good enough – for example, when the foreground object is as fiddly as this shopping cart. This operation calls for more specialized tools.

1 Start by placing the shopping cart – you'll find it at **bit.ly/136j70f**. Import it using **3D > New 3D Layer from File**.

2 Rotate the man so he more or less fits into the cart – it doesn't matter if a foot sticks out of the bottom – and hide the box.

3 We still need to see the cart, but we need to see the man more clearly. Reduce the opacity of the cart layer.

4 To reposition the man inside the cart, use **Edit > Puppet Warp**. This places a mesh on top of the man's layer.

5 Click inside the mesh to set **Pins** at the points to remain static: the knee, right foot, shoulder and midriff. I've marked the points here.

6 We can move any parts of the body with Puppet Warp. Click on the left foot, and drag it upward to move it inside the cart.

7 We can also rotate body parts. Click on the head and hold ⌥ *alt* as you drag to rotate the head around.

8 Hit *Enter* to apply the Puppet Warp step, and the grid will disappear as you return to normal operation.

9 When we now bring the shopping cart back to 100% opacity, the man fits neatly inside (right) – especially when we give him the support of the box. But this cart is far too complex to paint out on a mask: overleaf, we'll see how to solve this problem.

 Keyboard shortcuts   MAC WIN BOTH

10 Duplicate the cart layer, and drag the copy behind the man layer; then click the **eye** icon to hide it.

11 Click the **Scene** item in the **3D panel**, and the **Properties panel** will show this view. Click the **Cross Section** checkbox to activate it.

12 This is the result: half the model is hidden. The Cross Section process works by hiding everything on one side of the dividing line specified by the dialog.

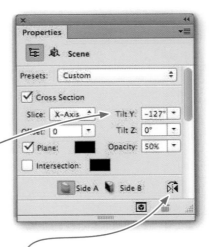

13 Drag the **Tilt Y** slider to turn the angle of the cut-off plane. As you can see here, the whole of the front half has been hidden.

14 That's all very well, but we want to hide the *back* half of the cart. So click the icon to flip the hidden side over.

15 That's better: now the back half is hidden, and the front half of the cart is fully visible.

16 It may take a while to fiddle with the settings to get the correct portion of the cart showing. We need to arrange it so that the none of the cart projects into the body of the man sitting inside. Here, I used a **Tilt Y** value of **-137°**.

17 With the front half complete, we can now reveal the copy of the full cart layer behind.

18 Here's the finished result. The man is now clearly sitting inside the cart. Just a few checkpoints:

- You'll need to hide the **Shadows** on the lights for the upper cart layer, or they'll interfere with the shadows cast by the bottom layer.

- You'll also need to paint some extra shadow as cast by the man sitting inside the cart.

- The best way to do this is to **Render** the lower cart layer, then **Select All** and do a **Copy Merged** operation ⌘ Shift C ctrl Shift C to produce a pixel-perfect copy of the rendered artwork. Paint your shadow on a new layer above this one, so you can modify it independently if necessary.

Keyboard shortcuts MAC WIN BOTH

Offsetting cross sections

THE CROSS SECTION part of the Properties panel includes several additional controls for twisting and manipulating cross sections. Here's another example of how to use this tool.

1 We're going to place a football helmet on this man: the helmet comes courtesy of The Archive from **digimation.com**.

2 You'll find the helmet already in place on the man, whose image you can download from **3DPhotoshop.net**.

3 Rotate the helmet to roughly the right position. Also, move the ground plane out of the way to avoid the shadow.

4 Use the **Cross Section** checkbox, as described on the previous pages, to cut the helmet in half.

5 Once again, the right approach here is to rotate the **Tilt Y** adjustment to turn the visible part of the helmet around. You can also uncheck the **Plane** box so that the visible gray plane of the cross section is hidden.

6 As you adjust the **Tilt Y** control, you'll see that the angle is now rather awkward; the whole helmet needs to be rotated a little more to fit the head. It's easier to see that now the back half of the helmet is missing.

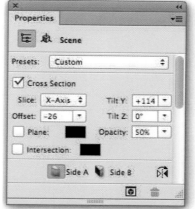

7 As you rotate the helmet, you'll see that the ear cushion is overlapping the man's cheek. We'll need to sort that out.

8 Rotating the **Tilt Y** control won't help here. Instead, drag the **Offset** slider to shift the position of the cross-section slice. You can see that the ear cushion is now removed from this half of the helmet.

9 View the back half of the helmet again by duplicating the 3D layer and moving it behind the figure of the man; select the **Scene** pane of the **Properties panel** for this version, and uncheck **Cross Section**.

10 As before, adding a shadow beneath the helmet helps to make it look like it's really on the figure. Make a new layer just above the man, using the man as a **Clipping Mask**, and paint the shadow on here.

11 If you want to get fancy, load the helmet layer as a selection and make a new layer, filled with black to match that selection, for the shadow of the bars. Use **Puppet Warp** to distort it to fit the contours of the face.

Integrating models into the scene

WHEN YOU PLACE a 3D object into a photographed environment, the challenge is always to make it appear as if it belongs in the space. There are several tricks we can use: using the background as an Image-Based Light, bringing foreground elements in front of the object, and matching lighting.

1 Here's our model car as we imported it into the Photoshop file. You can download this file, courtesy of Digimation, from **3DPhotoshop.net**.

2 The first step is to orient the model so it fits the scene. Be sure to move the *scene*, rather than the model, so you can be sure that the model remains sitting on the **Ground Plane**.

3 Trick number one: select a piece of the building on the background layer, copy it to a new layer and bring it to the front. When the model is integrated into the scene in this way, it will always look more authentic.

4 The next step is to fix the Image-Based Lighting (IBL). First, **Select All** on the Background layer and **Copy**. Select the **Environment** option at the top of the **3D panel**, then click the icon next to the IBL item at the top, and select **New Texture**.

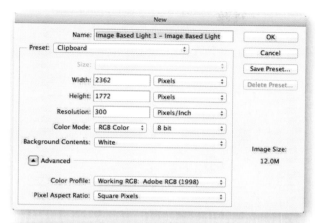

5 The standard new image dialog will appear, with the size set to the size of the image on the clipboard. Click **OK**.

6 The car will suddenly turn very bright. That's because the new texture is pure white.

7 Choose **Edit Texture** from the pop-up IBL menu, and **Paste** the image in. For speed, reduce the image size to about 800 pixels.

8 You'll now see the background overlaid on the car, completely surrounding it; a reduced view appears in the center.

9 Drag the center sphere to pan the image around, until you get a reflection in the car that you're happy with.

10 This is how the scene now looks when we click off the **Environment** pane. But this is just a rough preview.

11 Let's adjust the lighting to suit the scene. The main light comes from directly above, so select the **Light** pane in the **3D panel** and drag it up. It will help to reduce its Brightness slightly.

12 We can match the light coming from that lamp, as well. Add a new **Spot Light** from the icon at the bottom of the **3D panel**, and tint it yellow to match the light – but keep it at a low Brightness setting.

13 Time for a test render. And as you can see, the image is now far too bright. We need to tone down that IBL image.

14 Even though the Image-Based Lighting image is the same as the background, it's much too bright in this context. Choose **Edit Texture** from the pop-up IBL menu in the **Properties panel**.
   Rather than darkening the image, try this: add a new layer, and fill it with black. By setting the opacity of this layer to 50%, we can darken the layer without damaging it. **Save** to see the effect.

15 This is how the image now looks when rendered: the car is much more discreet, and the toned-down lighting works much better. But we still need to reduce the brightness, and increase the saturation.

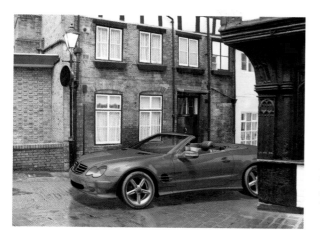

16 It can take a lot of experimentation with colors and test renders to get a good result. Here, I've chosen a darker, deeper color for the car by changing the swatch in the **Materials** pane of the **Properties panel**.

Because the road surface is wet, switch to the **Environment** pane and add a **Reflection** to the image

The finished image. The car blends in well with the background, and the lighting makes it look as if it belongs in the scene.

3D alignment with Vanishing Point

THE VANISHING POINT FILTER can be used to create 3D objects from photographs, as we saw on page 74. But it can also be used to define the perspective viewpoint of a scene, enabling us to position an object that sits flat on the ground, in exactly the right perspective.

1 I've chosen this photograph of an airport because its regular floor tiles will make the Vanishing Point procedure that much easier.

The model of the cart comes from the Digimation 3D Archive, and you'll find it already included in the file when you download it from **3DPhotoshop.net**.

2 To start the process off, hide the 3D model so you can see just the background, and choose **Vanishing Point** from the top of the **Filter** menu.

The aim is to mark four corners of a rectangular area within the image. The floor is obviously a good starting point.

3 There's no need to mark the whole floor – or, indeed, even a large part of it. Zoom in so you can see the tiles more clearly, and click once for each corner of an area defined by the lines between the tiles. You'll see this blue grid when you're done. Once you're happy with the placement, just click **OK**.

④ After applying the **Vanishing Point** filter, you'll see no difference in the image – but it's lurking in the background. Choose the **Camera** from the **3D panel**, then, in the **Properties panel**, change the **View** to the Vanishing Point Grid.

⑤ It's now most likely that your cart will change size and position as the camera shifts to its new position – it may well now be too large for the scene. But that will be easy to adjust now that the grid is in place.

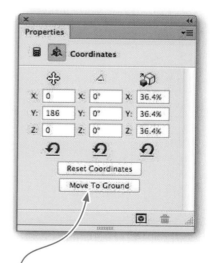

⑥ If you choose **View > Show > 3D Ground Plane**, you'll see the grid at ground level. It won't match the angles of the lines between the tiles, but it should match the overall perspective of the scene.

Drag the **Scale All** control in the middle of the **3D Axis** to make the whole cart smaller. Because this scales from the center, the cart will now be floating in space.

⑦ In the **Properties panel**, select the **Coordinates** option and click the **Move To Ground** button. This will drop the cart so it's sitting on the Ground Plane once more, as it should be.

8 It may take several tries at resizing the cart object – it's difficult to judge its scale without placing it on the **Ground Plane**, then sliding it around and resizing it again if the scale seems wrong.

Once it's the size you want, make sure the object remains selected, so you don't accidentally move the Ground Plane. To move it around, drag on either of the two visible faces, and rotate it by hovering the cursor over a vertical edge. You'll find you can "drive" it around the scene and it will remain in the correct perspective wherever you place it.

9 To make it belong more appropriately in the scene, you need to adjust the lighting. Click on the light icon and drag the virtual controller that appears in the middle of the screen.

The light in this image is hard to pin down, as so much of it is bouncing around from a variety of sources. However, if you look at the woman on the far left, you'll see that her shadow (as opposed to her reflection) is to her left, which places the light source on the right. It's relatively easy to simulate this by dragging the lighting control.

10 The next step is to set the Image-Based Lighting. Select the background and **Copy** it, then select **New Texture** from the pop-up menu next to the **IBL** thumbnail at the top of the **Properties panel**.

You'll be presented with a standard **New Document** dialog. As the size will already be the size of the image on the Clipboard, just click **OK**.

11 The image will now go far too bright, as a plain, white **IBL** will have been applied. To fix this, choose **Edit Texture** from the same pop-up menu as in the previous step, and **Paste** the background image in place.

12 Here's how the scene will now look: remember that the overlay shows the inside of the **IBL** texture as wrapped around a sphere, whereas the ball in the middle shows the same texture wrapped around the outside of a smaller sphere for reference.

Drag the ball until you site the reflection in a position that looks appropriate.

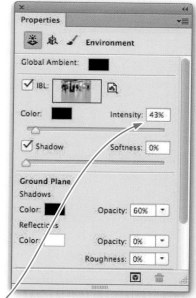

13 With the **IBL** applied, you'll probably find that the whole cart now looks far too bright. You can try darkening the image, as we did on page 210, or you can just reduce the **Intensity** of the light in the **Properties panel**.

Here, I've used an **Intensity** setting of just over 40% to achieve the right level of brightness

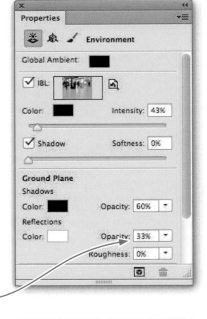

14 With the lighting more or less right, we can add a reflection. Select **Environment** at the top of the **3D panel**, then increase the opacity of the Reflections setting in the **Properties panel**. The amount you choose is somewhat hit and miss; try a test area render to check it out ●

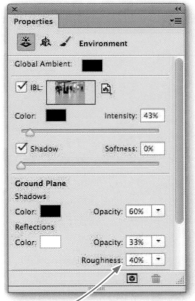

15 The opacity of the reflection may now be correct, but it's far too deep: look at how the reflections of the people fade away and merge into the floor. Experiment with the **Roughness** setting to reduce the extent of the reflection, which will adjust the distance they extend ●

16 The shadow is also too strong, and too crisp. You can make it less sharp by increasing the **Shadow Softness** value in the **Environment** pane of the **Properties panel**.

17 Try a full render to see how it looks. Here, the cart is a little dark; I increased the **Intensity** of the **IBL** slider in the **Properties panel** to brighten it all up a little.

In the final render, the cart looks very much part of the scene, as if it truly belonged in this airport.

Refracting the background

WE'VE SEEN HOW to make objects transparent, and how to make them reflect each other. Working with photographic backgrounds, though, is a different matter: the background itself has to be part of the scene in order for 3D objects to work with them.

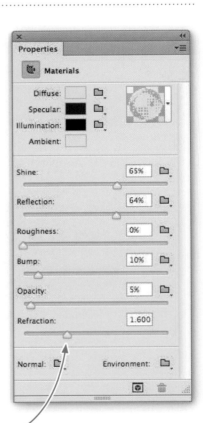

1 This glass has been made by revolving a drawn profile, as we saw on page 30. This has then been placed on a table in front of a photographed background. The issue now is to make the glass transparent.

2 You can choose a glass texture from the presets in the **Properties panel**, or you can make one yourself: it's easy to do, simply combining a low opacity with a degree of refraction. A value of around 1.6 works well

3 An **Opacity** setting of just 5% means that the glass is now almost invisible against that background.

But we've encountered a problem: the profile used to draw the shape of the glass remains visible once the glass around it has been made transparent. We need to work out why this is, and fix the problem.

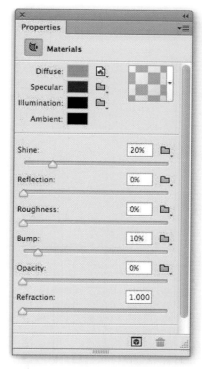

4 It turns out to be a simple fix. When we clicked on the glass to set the **Opacity**, we were only affecting the **Extrusion Material**. If we select the **Front** and **Back Inflation Materials** in the **3D panel**, we can set their **Opacity** to zero to make them invisible.

5 Let's try rendering the scene, to see what happens now that all parts of the glass are fully transparent.

It's a little disappointing. The glass is transparent, right enough, but what about the refraction we were expecting? We can still see right through it.

The issue here is that the photographed background is not linked to the 3D object in any way. It's a wholly separate layer. We need to bring the two together for there to be any interaction between them.

6 We need to make the background into a 3D layer. So to do this, select it and choose **3D Postcard** as the object type in the **3D panel**, then click **Create**.

7 As you'd expect, you don't see any immediate difference when you turn the background into a 3D postcard. That's because it's oriented exactly the same as the original, flat on and facing us directly. When you try another test render, though, you'll find that the glass still fails to refract the background.

8 The problem is that although the glass and the background are both 3D objects, they remain on separate layers.

9 Drag the Background object above the glass in the **Layers panel**, then **Merge** the two layers together ⌘ E *ctrl* E. The background will probably come out halfway through the table; move it back in the scene, and enlarge it until it fits the space once more.

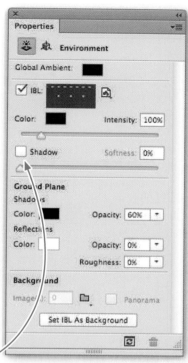

10 When you now render the scene, you'll find that the background comes out very dark. That's due to the **Shadow**, set in the **Environment** pane. This checkbox controls shading on the background, as opposed to shadows cast directly by a light.

Because the background we're working with here is a flat photograph rather than purely on the ground plane, that shadow will only get in the way. Uncheck the shadow to remove it

11 You don't have to get very far through the next test render before you discover another issue: the edges of the glass are showing transparent pixels, and not in a good sense.

What's going on here is that the glass is duly refracting the background, as requested. But the background image is now a 3D Postcard, a separate object in its own right; and the side of the glass is bending the light so much that it's attempting to show pixels that are outside the scope of the Postcard object.

12 In order to catch refractions from those extreme areas, we need to set the photographic image as a new Background within the 3D scene.

First, open and copy the original Background layer. Then select **Environment** at the top of the **3D panel**, then switch to the **Properties panel**. Right at the bottom, you'll find the **Background** section. From the pop-up menu, select **New Texture**

13 As before, when adding new textures, it will begin with white. You need to choose **Edit Texture** from the same menu and paste in the background.

The finished render is below: you can see how, eventually, we managed to get the glass to both refract and reflect the background.

PART FOUR

Special projects

15 More techniques

IN THE ORIGINAL RENDER for the opening illustration for this section, the glass came out far too dull. But it had taken all night to render; I didn't want to have to do it all over again. However – this is Photoshop, after all, so we can use any of the Photoshop techniques to fix a visual problem.

1 After doing a **Select All**, I used **Edit > Copy Merged** followed by **Paste** to make a flat copy of the render.

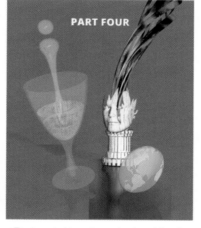

2 I wanted to make a selection of the glass – but there was too much in the way. I deleted the ground and text elements.

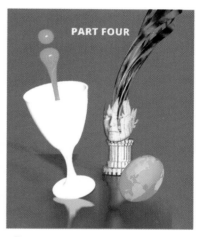

3 To ensure a good selection, I changed the opacity of the glass (and the liquid) to 100%.

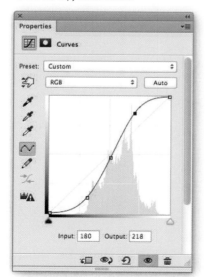

4 I loaded up the remaining parts of the 3D layer as a selection by holding ⌘ ctrl and clicking on the layer's thumbnail in the **3D panel**. I then used the **Lasso tool**, holding ⌘ ⌥ ctrl alt, to loop around the glass so only it was selected.

With the selection now made, I created a new **Curves Adjustment Layer**, and the selection behaved as a mask; I dragged in the curve to increase the contrast of the selection.

5 The result: a much more dramatic shot of the glass. Sometimes, it's easier to cheat than to repeat a lengthy render.

Keyboard shortcuts   MAC WIN BOTH

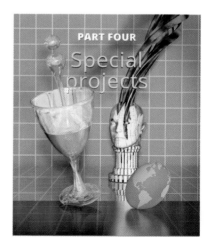

Making it move

AS WELL AS RENDERING still images, Photoshop can make objects, lights and even the camera move over time – and then render out movies showing the motion. By marking keyframes, we set the points at which an object changes speed or direction; Photoshop will figure out smooth motion between the keyframes.

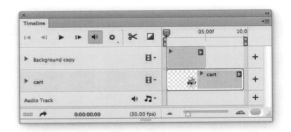

1 Start by choosing **Timeline** from the **Window** menu, if it isn't already open. Click the **Create Video Timeline** button to make a new movie track.

2 The Timeline window will now show all the layers in your document. The *Background copy* I've created here is a duplicate of those bars in the bottom left of the picture, copied to the front.

3 Open the *Cart* arrow. At the bottom is the **objMesh** control: click the **watch** icon to animate the layer, and click the **diamond** between the arrows to make a keyframe.

4 Move the cart to the starting position, using the usual 3D controls. Its position will be recorded at that keyframe location.

5 Drag the **time marker** a few seconds along, and move the cart to its new position. Then click the **keyframe marker** again.

6 You can rotate the model as well as dragging it, and Photoshop will produce a smooth motion between keyframe markers.

How to use the Timeline window

Use the **Playback** controls to play and step through the movie

You can control every aspect of the 3D scene, not just the object's angle and position

Change the length of time a layer is visible by dragging the ends

Drag the **Time** marker to move to a specific point in the movie. The current time location is indicated by a vertical red line

Keyframes are shown in the timeline as diamonds. They're the points at which an event takes place

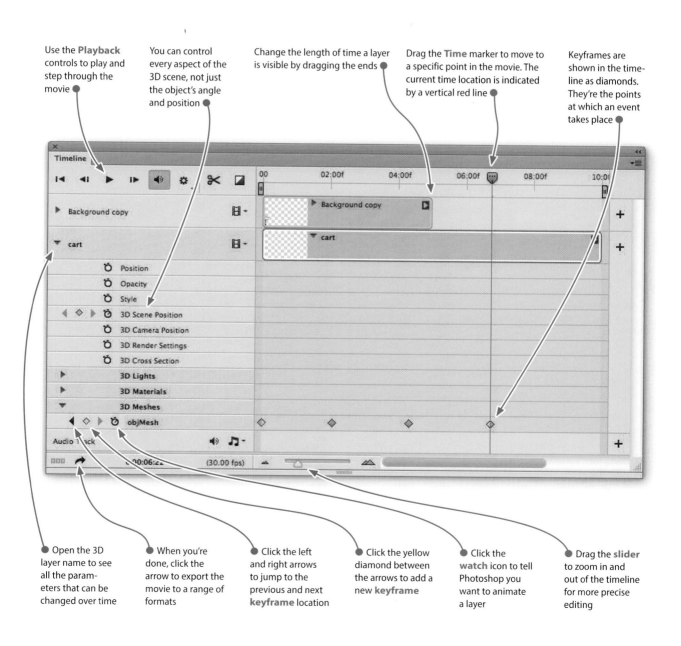

Open the 3D layer name to see all the parameters that can be changed over time

When you're done, click the arrow to export the movie to a range of formats

Click the left and right arrows to jump to the previous and next **keyframe** location

Click the yellow diamond between the arrows to add a new **keyframe**

Click the **watch** icon to tell Photoshop you want to animate a layer

Drag the **slider** to zoom in and out of the timeline for more precise editing

Book building

MANY DESIGNERS work with book covers at some point in their careers. And they're always presented to the client as flat artwork – or they go to extreme lengths to print the covers out, wrap them around a real book and then photograph them. Wouldn't it be convenient if there were another way to do it?

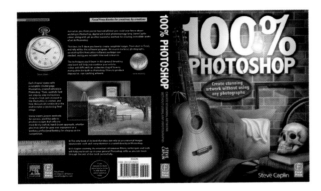

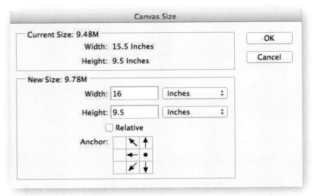

1 This is the cover for my own book **100% Photoshop**, complete with back cover and spine. The cover measures 7½ inches wide by 9½ inches high, more or less, and the spine is half an inch thick.

Actually, the cover is more like 7⅜ by 9⅝, but to keep things simple I resized it using the **Image Size** dialog. This would save more complex calculations later.

2 To make the texture for the book model, it's necessary to make the canvas wider so it can include a texture for the pages at the edge. The front and back covers between them add up to 15 inches, and adding the spine makes 15½ inches. So to add that extra half inch, use the **Edit > Canvas Size** dialog to make the width 16 inches, anchoring the cover on the right side to add the extra space on the left.

3 To make the page texture, start with a selection the same size as the spine, on a new layer, and fill it with a pale brown. Make a selection 1 pixel thick in this texture and fill it with a darker brown, then hold ⌥ *alt* as you use the cursor keys to nudge it 1 pixel away from the first. This will make a copy of the selection.

Release the keys and nudge again, to move the new stripe so as to leave some distance between it and the original. Repeat this process, occasionally making double-width stripes and occasionally leaving double-width spaces. The random spacing will make the pages look more realistic.

4 This is how the book cover will look when the page texture is in place. **Save** the document, so it can be loaded later; and also save the page texture as a document on its own, as we'll need to use that to create the top and bottom page edges.

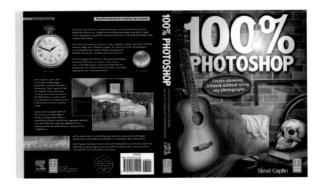

Keyboard shortcuts   MAC WIN BOTH

5 With the texture made, we can now start to build the model. Make a new Photoshop document slightly larger than the height of the book – in this case, I made one about 10 inches square. I used a resolution of 150 lines per inch, but you can increase this if you like.

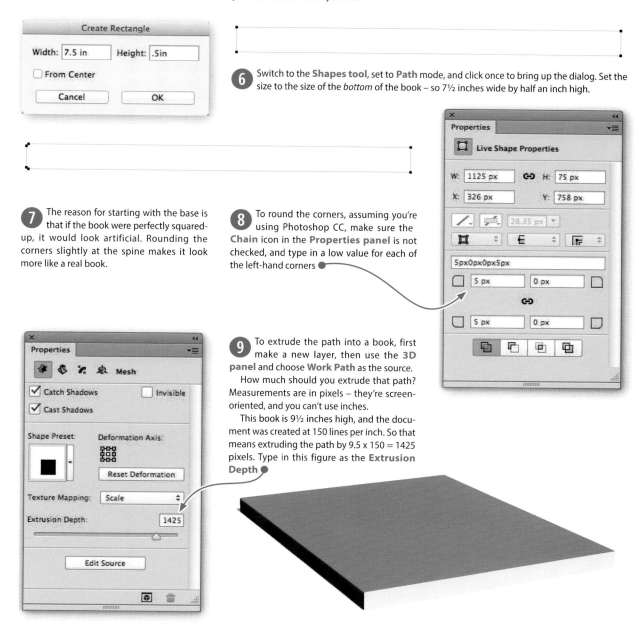

6 Switch to the **Shapes tool**, set to **Path** mode, and click once to bring up the dialog. Set the size to the size of the *bottom* of the book – so 7½ inches wide by half an inch high.

7 The reason for starting with the base is that if the book were perfectly squared-up, it would look artificial. Rounding the corners slightly at the spine makes it look more like a real book.

8 To round the corners, assuming you're using Photoshop CC, make sure the **Chain** icon in the **Properties panel** is not checked, and type in a low value for each of the left-hand corners ●

9 To extrude the path into a book, first make a new layer, then use the **3D panel** and choose **Work Path** as the source.

How much should you extrude that path? Measurements are in pixels – they're screen-oriented, and you can't use inches.

This book is 9½ inches high, and the document was created at 150 lines per inch. So that means extruding the path by 9.5 x 150 = 1425 pixels. Type in this figure as the **Extrusion Depth** ●

10 Now that the book has been modeled, we can add the texture to it. Click on the book's surface, then again, so that the **Materials** pane of the **Properties panel** comes into view.

From the pop-up menu next to the **Diffuse** item at the top, choose **Load Texture**. You'll be presented with the standard **Open** dialog; navigate to the saved cover.

11 The cover is likely to come out upside-down, due to the way Photoshop handles textures. Use the **Coordinates** pane of the **Properties panel** to turn it the right way up, by rotating the **X** value

12 The texture wraps around the front, spine and back OK, but there's no texture on the ends of those pages – the bottom side is completely blank.

Select the bottom side of the book, and use the same process as in step 10 to apply the page texture saved at the beginning.

13 Rather surprisingly, the texture doesn't produce a perfect match for the book sides. Instead, it has been rotated 90° and greatly enlarged. Photoshop does do strange things with textures sometimes.

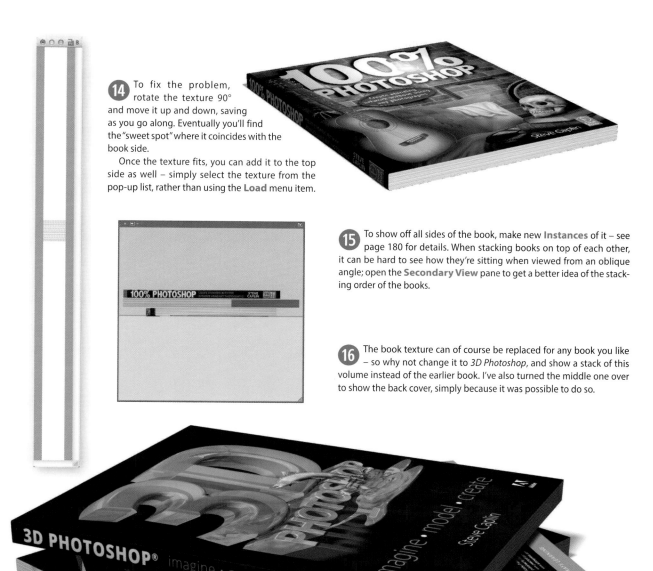

14 To fix the problem, rotate the texture 90° and move it up and down, saving as you go along. Eventually you'll find the "sweet spot" where it coincides with the book side.

Once the texture fits, you can add it to the top side as well – simply select the texture from the pop-up list, rather than using the **Load** menu item.

15 To show off all sides of the book, make new **Instances** of it – see page 180 for details. When stacking books on top of each other, it can be hard to see how they're sitting when viewed from an oblique angle; open the **Secondary View** pane to get a better idea of the stacking order of the books.

16 The book texture can of course be replaced for any book you like – so why not change it to *3D Photoshop*, and show a stack of this volume instead of the earlier book. I've also turned the middle one over to show the back cover, simply because it was possible to do so.

Dancing the twist

MERGING PHOTOGRAPHS and 3D objects doesn't have to be just about creating photorealistic images. We can use Photoshop's ability to generate any object we can imagine to produce striking fantasy scenes. Here, we'll look at a method of wrapping a girl up in a swirling, twisting, organic form.

  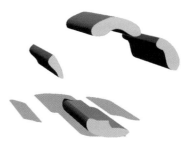

1 This photograph of a girl comes courtesy of **absolutvision.com**. You'll find the image ready for download on **3DPhotoshop.net**.

Hide the girl layer for now, while we build the 3D object.

2 Make a new layer, and draw some random shapes on it. Because we want to be able to see the girl inside the twists, I've made these widely spaced (to leaves gaps between them), and with a large hole in the middle. This should allow space for the girl to float inside.

3 Open the **3D panel** and, with the Source set to Selected Layer, **Extrude** the layer. As you'd expect, it turns into a regular extruded 3D layer.

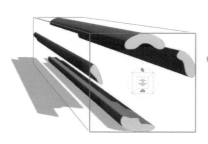 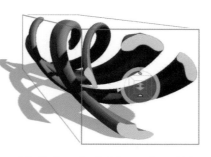 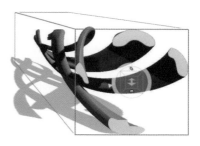

4 Click on the layer, and press **V** to open the **Head-Up Controls**. First, click in the middle to **Extrude** the shape as far as it will go into the distance.

The maximum allowed extrusion is 2500 pixels, which isn't quite far enough – but we can always stretch the shape later.

5 Next, use the **Twist** control to twirl the object into a spiral. Grab the control and drag it around the circle to achieve this effect.

6 A small amount of **Taper** will make the twist smaller at one end.

There's no need to get these settings exactly right at this stage, as they can always be changed later on. But it is useful to have some sort of shape to play with, even if it's going to be adjusted further down the line.

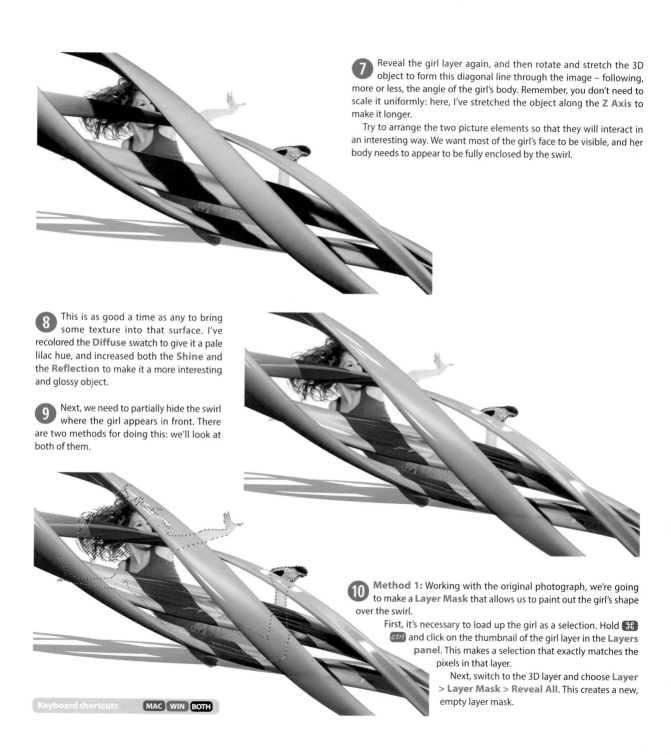

7 Reveal the girl layer again, and then rotate and stretch the 3D object to form this diagonal line through the image – following, more or less, the angle of the girl's body. Remember, you don't need to scale it uniformly: here, I've stretched the object along the **Z Axis** to make it longer.

Try to arrange the two picture elements so that they will interact in an interesting way. We want most of the girl's face to be visible, and her body needs to appear to be fully enclosed by the swirl.

8 This is as good a time as any to bring some texture into that surface. I've recolored the **Diffuse** swatch to give it a pale lilac hue, and increased both the **Shine** and the **Reflection** to make it a more interesting and glossy object.

9 Next, we need to partially hide the swirl where the girl appears in front. There are two methods for doing this: we'll look at both of them.

10 **Method 1:** Working with the original photograph, we're going to make a **Layer Mask** that allows us to paint out the girl's shape over the swirl.

First, it's necessary to load up the girl as a selection. Hold ⌘ **ctrl** and click on the thumbnail of the girl layer in the **Layers panel**. This makes a selection that exactly matches the pixels in that layer.

Next, switch to the 3D layer and choose **Layer > Layer Mask > Reveal All**. This creates a new, empty layer mask.

Keyboard shortcuts **MAC** **WIN** **BOTH**

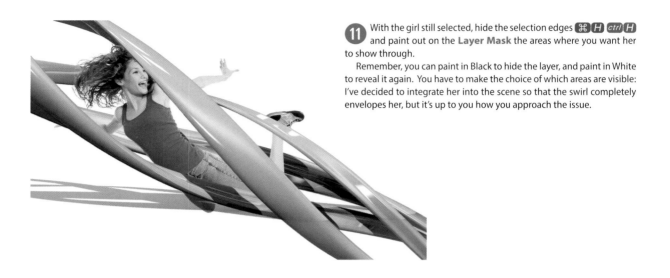

11 With the girl still selected, hide the selection edges ⌘ H ctrl H and paint out on the **Layer Mask** the areas where you want her to show through.

Remember, you can paint in Black to hide the layer, and paint in White to reveal it again. You have to make the choice of which areas are visible: I've decided to integrate her into the scene so that the swirl completely envelopes her, but it's up to you how you approach the issue.

12 This is the final render. I've hidden the shadows, as they looked artificial only on the swirl itself, and not on the girl. In addition, they were showing on the **Ground Plane**, which was getting in the way. Turning them off in the **Lighting** pane made sense.

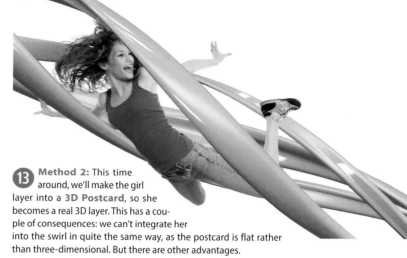

13 **Method 2:** This time around, we'll make the girl layer into a **3D Postcard**, so she becomes a real 3D layer. This has a couple of consequences: we can't integrate her into the swirl in quite the same way, as the postcard is flat rather than three-dimensional. But there are other advantages.

14 The main benefit of making the girl into a 3D Postcard is that we can now introduce such elements as **Transparency** and **Refraction** into the swirl. In addition, the swirl now reflects the girl's body, which integrates her much better into the scene, as the final render below demonstrates. Also, we no longer need that **Layer Mask**, so it can be discarded.

Filling a wine glass

THE OPENING ILLUSTRATION for this section features a wine glass half full of wine, with a giant droplet of wine about to leap out of it. The effect is remarkably easy to achieve, by duplicating the original object and then modifying the source path.

1 In this version of the glass, I've set the opacity at higher than I'd normally choose so it can be seen clearly on the page.

2 As with all transparent objects, the preview gives only the vaguest idea of how it will look; here's the same object rendered.

3 Use the pop-up menu to **Duplicate** the glass. Don't create an **Instance**, as we only want to adjust one of them.

4 Select the new glass and, in the Properties pane, select **Edit Source**. It will open in a new window.

5 Switch to the **Direct Selection tool**, and select all the anchor points on the path except those inside the glass (left). The selected points will be shown filled with black.

6 Use *Backspace* to delete all those selected points. You'll be left with just the two points inside the glass, joined by a curve.

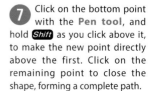

7 Click on the bottom point with the **Pen tool**, and hold *Shift* as you click above it, to make the new point directly above the first. Click on the remaining point to close the shape, forming a complete path.

8 Close and **Save** the path window, and you'll be able to see the new object as a darker shape inside the original.

9 Use the **Properties panel** to change the **Diffuse** color to a deep red. Above right is a rendered version of the glass.

10 You're not limited to just closing off the path – you can make it any shape you wish for dramatic effect.

I've extended the path upward to make the flying droplet, and I've also added a ripple on the left to make the surface of the wine more interesting.

11 Here's how the glass now looks when the **Source** path is saved.

Again, the preview doesn't do it justice; when a background is added, the whole object looks much better in the final render.

Complex material matching

ONE OF THE BASIC objects provided by Photoshop is a wine bottle, which is composed of three separate 3D models – the bottle itself, the label, and the foil cap. But we can create the entire bottle as a single object, which gives us more flexibility over the size and placement of labels; it just takes a bit of working out.

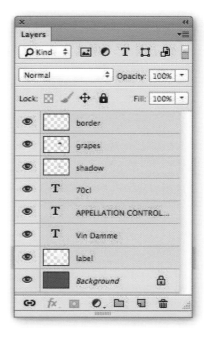

1 This basic bottle shape was made by revolving a path. You can download this object from **3DPhotoshop. net**.

2 Add a new **Diffuse** texture, using the pop-up menu at the top of the **Materials** pane of the **Properties panel**. As before, 1000 x 1000 pixels is a good starting size.

　　Because the default new texture is blank, the bottle will turn completely white.

3 When you choose **Edit Texture** from the same pop-up menu, the texture will open in a new window. Fill this window with a dark bottle green and **Save** the file, and the bottle will turn green.

4 Design your label inside this texture window. When you've finished the design, select all the layers that make up the label, and choose **Layer > Smart Objects > Convert to Smart Object**. This is an important step, as we'll see.

5 When you now **Save** the texture file, you'll see the label appearing on the bottle – but it's very likely to be highly distorted, and in an unlikely position.

The process of mapping a flat texture onto a three-dimensional surface is a complex one, and Photoshop doesn't always place picture elements where you'd expect them to be.

6 The best way to find the right location for the label is simply to move it around within the texture, using ⌘S ctrl S to **Save** the file each time you move it.

Here, the label is more or less in the right place – but it has been rotated and grossly distorted out of shape.

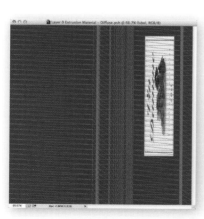

7 It can help to view the underlying grid – choose **View > Show > UV Overlay** to see the grid on the texture. The closer the blue lines, the more the texture is bent over a curved part of the model.

Using Free Transform ⌘T ctrl T, rotate the label and stretch it so it fits the bottle. It may take a huge distortion, as seen here.

8 Because the label has been so distorted, it now appears on the bottle at low resolution. But we can fix that: simply use the **Image Size** dialog to increase the size of the texture, to 2000 x 2000 pixels.

This is one of the big advantages of converting the label to a Smart Object: it will scale up to remove the pixelation effect.

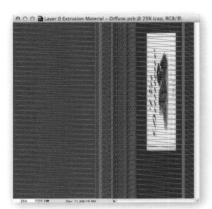

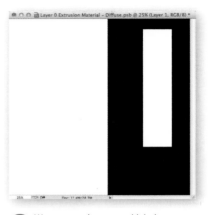

9   Make another new layer inside the texture file, draw a rectangular selection, and fill it with red to make the cap. You can see where to draw it, more or less, by the arrangement of the blue **UV Overlay** lines. **Save** the file to apply the texture to the model.

10   We can use the cap and label to create an **Opacity** map. In the texture document, make a new layer and fill it with black. Then load the label and cap by holding ⌘ *ctrl* and clicking on their layer thumbnails, and fill the selections with white. Copy this layer, and hide it on the **Diffuse** material; then make a new **Opacity** texture, and paste it in place.

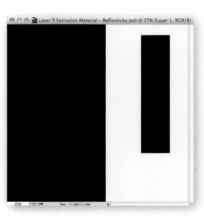

11   The pure black of the opacity map made the bottle completely transparent – in the last step, it disappeared entirely.

To bring back some of the visibility, lighten the whole opacity texture so the black becomes gray, and the bottle will reappear. The lighter the gray, the more opaque the bottle.

12   We can add some reflection and shine to the bottle as well. It's OK to get a little shine off the cap and label, but we don't want them to reflect anything. So make a new texture for the **Reflection**, and paste in the same texture; this time, though, use **Image > Adjustments > Invert** so that the white area marks the reflective region.

13 You can duplicate the bottle and rotate it to provide an empty one behind the first bottle.

Here, I've also added some wine inside the standing bottle, using the same technique as described on page 236. I also reduced the size of the wine slightly, so it would sit inside the bottle rather than interfering with the outside.

14 Because the label was turned into a Smart Object, it's easy to change it. Open the **Diffuse** texture, then double-click the label layer to open it in a new window. When you're done, first **Save** the Smart Object, then **Save** the texture itself.

Simulating multiple objects

THE MORE OBJECTS you add to a 3D scene, the more complex the scene becomes – and the longer it takes to make any changes, or to produce a render. But it's possible to make a single object that appears to be constructed of many parts, as we'll see in this railings example.

1 This rainy London street features a cobbled road that meets the curb of the sidewalk. We're going to make an additional set of railings along the curb line.

2 To make the railings, you don't need to draw each individual pole on its own – you can make Photoshop do the work. Open the **Brush panel**, and set a small brush with 100% **Hardness**. Then adjust the **Spacing**: I've used a value of 500 to get these wide gaps

3 Make a new layer, and use the **Pen tool** to draw a path consisting of a straight line, a curve around 90°, and then another, shorter line. This simulates the way the sidewalk wraps around the street, following the curve of the curb.

4 With the path still active, select the **Brush tool** and hit `Enter`. The brush will "stroke" the path, following the line of the path and painting along it. Because the brush was defined with a wide spacing, it leaves even gaps along its length as it follows the path.

5 Now for the bars that join the railings. Make another new layer, and reduce the spacing of the brush again (or just select a standard, hard-edged brush). Again, with the path still selected, press `Enter` and the path will be stroked with the new brush. This time, it will produce a solid iine.

6 To set the perspective of the scene, use the **Vanishing Point filter** as described on page 212. There's no easy grid on the ground to follow, but you can get some clues by following the lines between the paving slabs, and the front edge of the curb.

7 Switch to the layer on which you drew the dots for the railings, and in the **3D panel**, create a new **3D Extrusion** from the layer. It will come out looking straight down on the railings, as seen here; rotate them 90° around the **X Axis** so they're standing vertically.

8 Switch the current camera view to the **Vanishing Point Grid**, and you should find the scene more or less lines up with the background. It may take some manual fiddling to get it right. Use the **Head-Up Controls** to move and rotate the railings into position.

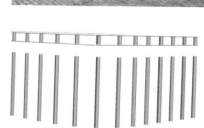

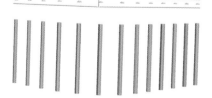

9 Now for the spikes. Duplicate the railings inside the 3D layer, and move the copy up out of the way – reduce the **Extrusion** amount so you can see what you're doing more clearly.

10 Set the **Extrusion** to zero and, in the **Properties panel**, move to the **Cap** pane and increase the **Width** of the bevel. You can also increase the **Angle**, up to a maximum of 85%, to make a spike.

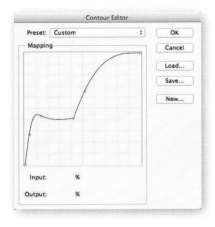

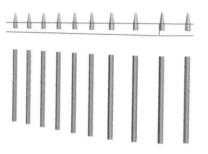

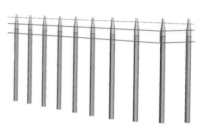

11 Click the **Contour** thumbnail in the **Cap** pane of the **Properties panel**, and click and drag points on the line to make a curve. You can see the shape of the spike changing as you work.

12 This is the result of that operation: the plain cylindrical extrusion has now been transformed into a rounded spike – and it's been applied to all the railings in the set at the same time.

13 Now that the spikes are complete, you can move them back down so that they meet the original railings.

14 Return to the layer created in step 5, and **Extrude** the layer as before. Once again, it will come out lying flat on its side; rotate it 90°, and reduce the **Extrusion** to a very small value.

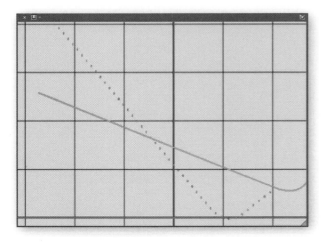

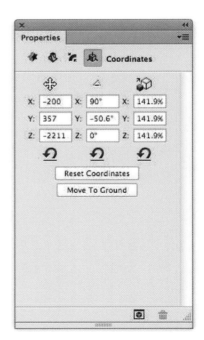

15 Merge the new rail layer down into the railings layer, so that all the 3D elements are in a single layer.

To align the rail with the railings, you'll find it easier if you open the **Secondary View** and keep this open as you rotate it. It may be hard to reach the **Head-Up Display**, so instead drag on the **X**, **Y** and **Z** letters in the **Coordinates** pane of the **Properties panel** to change the angle and location.

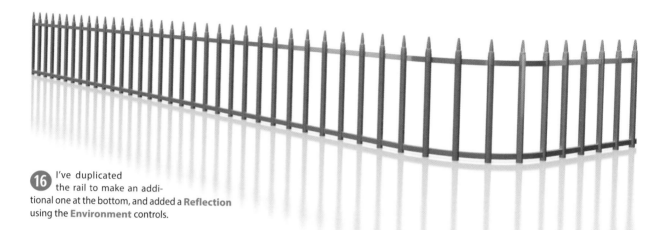

16 I've duplicated the rail to make an additional one at the bottom, and added a **Reflection** using the **Environment** controls.

After the final render was complete, I added a Layer Mask to the railings layer. On this mask I painted out the reflection in the face of the curb stones, as there would be no reflection in this vertical side; and I also painted out the crooked post so it could poke through the railings.

Divide and rule

PHOTOSHOP'S ABILITY TO CREATE 3D models from photographs is extraordinary, as we've seen. But sometimes those photographs don't lend themselves to a single 3D operation; to get the best results, we sometimes need to divide the image up into its constituent parts first.

1 This photograph of a stuffed, mounted fish has been cut out with the background removed. You can download it from **3DPhotoshop.net**.

2 Here's the first go at turning it into a 3D object, using the **Inflation** method as discussed in Chapter 4. Viewed from the side, it looks reasonably convincing.

3 Once we spin the fish around, though, it looks more like an inflated balloon. Those fins are far too thick – a fish could never swim with fins like that.

4 The solution is to go back to the original photograph, and select the fins (best to use the **Pen tool** to get a smooth selection). Use **Layer > Layer Via Cut** to cut the fins to a layer of their own.

5 The two fins at the bottom should be sticking out at an angle, because they're actually pairs of fins, one on each side. Select them and cut them to two separate layers of their own.

6 Go back to the fish layer, and use the **Clone tool** to patch over the original fin at the front – and to patch the place where the lower fin has been removed, which left a hole behind.

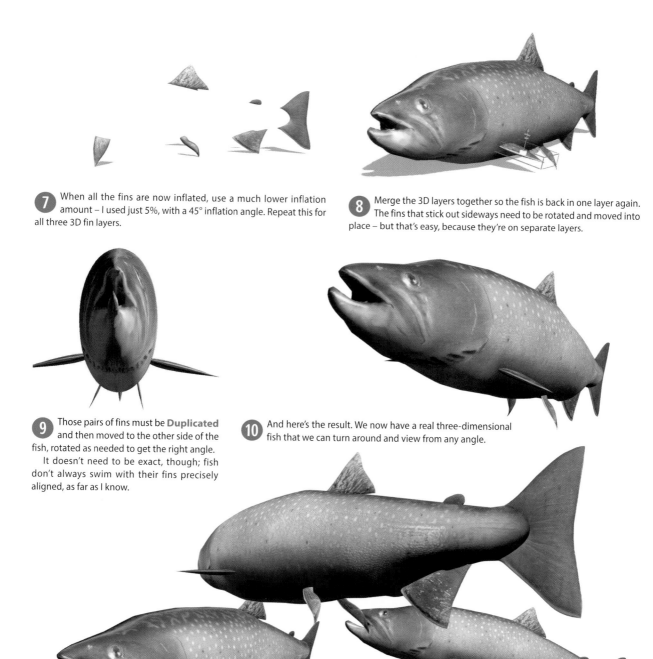

7 When all the fins are now inflated, use a much lower inflation amount – I used just 5%, with a 45° inflation angle. Repeat this for all three 3D fin layers.

8 Merge the 3D layers together so the fish is back in one layer again. The fins that stick out sideways need to be rotated and moved into place – but that's easy, because they're on separate layers.

9 Those pairs of fins must be **Duplicated** and then moved to the other side of the fish, rotated as needed to get the right angle.

It doesn't need to be exact, though; fish don't always swim with their fins precisely aligned, as far as I know.

10 And here's the result. We now have a real three-dimensional fish that we can turn around and view from any angle.

Index